BUILD
LLM APPLICATIONS
LOCALLY

with Python, Ollama, LangChain, and Gradio

A HANDS-ON GUIDE

Prabir Guha

For permission requests, write to the author at:

prabir.guha@nxgen.ai

First Edition, 2025

ISBN: 979-8-28174-827-8

This book is dedicated to my wife Runa.

TABLE OF CONTENTS

Introduction

"Any sufficiently advanced technology is indistinguishable from magic." What Arthur C. Clarke, the author of 2001 Space Odyssey, famously observed is especially relevant in the era of Large Language Models (LLMs). These sophisticated AI systems can generate human-like text, write code, compose music, and even assist in medical diagnoses—capabilities that may seem almost magical to those unfamiliar with the underlying complex technology driving them. However, this magic is not the result of conscious awareness but rather the culmination of decades of progress in Artificial Intelligence (AI), Natural Language Processing (NLP), and Deep Learning.

Evolution of Natural Language Processing

The journey of NLP began in the 1950s and 1960s with simple rule-based systems and statistical approaches before transitioning to neural network-based Large Language Models (LLMs) that are in use today. Early advancements included bag-of-words, TF_IDF, N-gram models, and recurrent neural networks (RNNs), which, while effective in limited capacities, struggled with long-term dependencies in terms of their ability to retain and utilize information from earlier parts of a text when generating or interpreting long sentences.

What Are LLMs?

Large Language Models (LLMs) are AI Systems trained on vast datasets of human language. These language datasets include the content of Wikipedia, scientific papers from the arXiv repository, collection of biomedical and life sciences literature from PubMed, social media data from Twitter and Reddit, collection of eleven thousand books from BooksCorpus, collection of public domain books from the Project Gutenberg, and many other sources.

LLMs are deep learning models constructed from Neural Networks that store knowledge as built-in parameters, that is, computer programs that translate text and grammar into numbers, store them in internal data structures (parameters), and act on them to analyze and generate new text with remarkable fluency and coherence. LLMs can perform various tasks by leveraging billions of parameters and extensive training on diverse sources, from answering complex questions to summarizing large documents and translating languages. The term "Large" in these models refers to the vast number of internal parameters, which are in the hundreds of billions, and the extensive data sets comprising trillions of words that were used for their training.

Neural Network-based deep learning models are versatile and have been able to perform human tasks like Object Recognition (with remarkable success) and Natural Language Processing (with less success) for over a decade. However, the stunning breakthrough in natural language processing capabilities that we are witnessing today with the LLMs came about with the introduction of the Transformer architecture, a variation of the deep learning architecture tailored for Natural Language Processing. The Transformer architecture for natural language processing was introduced in the seminal paper by **Vaswani et al. (2017), "Attention Is All You Need."** The paper fundamentally reshaped the field of natural language processing.

Overview of Major LLMs

Several major LLMs have played pivotal roles in recent language AI advancements:

- GPT (Generative Pre-trained Transformer): Developed by OpenAI, with iterations like GPT-3, GPT-4, and GPT-5, excelling in text generation and reasoning tasks.
- BERT (Bidirectional Encoder Representations from Transformers): Google's model is designed for deep bidirectional understanding of text and is widely used for search and NLP applications.
- LLaMA (Large Language Model Meta AI): A more efficient and open-source alternative to traditional LLMs, designed by Meta for research and practical applications. In this book, we use llama 3.1, freely available from the Ollama repository, as our learning platform.
- Gemini, Claude, and Mistral: Other notable models that bring unique optimizations and specializations to the LLM landscape.

Applications and Impact of LLMs

LLMs are transforming industries by enabling powerful automation and augmenting human capabilities in many domains. Some of them are:

- Text Generation: LLMs can generate coherent and contextually appropriate text, making them useful for content creation and automated reporting.
- Question Answering: With a deep understanding of context, LLMs excel at retrieving and generating accurate responses to complex queries.
- Code Generation: By understanding programming languages, these models assist developers in writing and debugging code.
- Specialized Applications: LLMs are increasingly used in domains such as healthcare and law, where they help analyze complex documents, support decision-making, and improve information retrieval.
- Multimodal Processing: Beyond text, modern systems are beginning to integrate image, audio, and text processing, broadening the scope of NLP applications.

The potential of LLMs is immense. At the end of this journey, you will understand how LLMs function and, more importantly, how to use them in your work. We list below what is in each chapter:

1: How Large Language Models (LLMs) Work: Traces the evolution of natural language processing (NLP) from early rule-based systems like ELIZA to today's transformer-based LLMs such as GPT and BERT. Early systems relied on fixed rules and grammars, a major breakthrough came with deep learning and the Transformer architecture, which introduced self-attention to model language context more effectively. The chapter explains how modern LLMs are built using encoders, decoders, or both (encoder-decoder models), each suited for specific tasks such as understanding, generating, or translating text.

2: Install and Configure the Ollama software on Your Workstation: Provides a comprehensive guide to installing, configuring, and using Ollama, a lightweight framework for running Large Language Models (LLMs) like LLaMA and Mistral locally on a workstation. It highlights the benefits of local LLM execution—such as privacy, offline use, no API costs, and low latency—compared to cloud-based services.

3: First LLM Application with Python: Introduces how to build your first Python application that interacts with a locally hosted Large Language Model

(LLM) using the Ollama framework. It guides you through installing prerequisites like Python 3.10+, necessary Python libraries, and the Ollama server running the llama3.1 model. Two methods are demonstrated for interacting with the LLM: HTTP requests with the requests Python module and the official Ollama Python library for direct model access. The chapter emphasizes best practices like setting up a virtual environment for managing Python dependencies and optionally leveraging GPU acceleration for performance.

4: Prompting: Emphasizes the importance of prompting in Large Language Model (LLM) applications, explaining how well-crafted prompts directly impact the quality and relevance of model responses. Prompting acts as the communication bridge between users and models like llama3.1, guiding the LLM to interpret instructions and produce desired output. Various techniques—such as role-based, instruction-based, chain-of-thought, and few-shot prompting—are introduced to improve the LLM's performance.

5: LangChain - Framework for Building LLM Applications: Introduces LangChain as a powerful, open-source framework for building advanced LLM-based applications by chaining prompts, memory, and logic. It simplifies LLM integration and supports prompt management, tool use, and context-aware conversations.

6: LLM Application Usecases: Illustrates the versatility of LangChain library by showcasing four practical Python programs that demonstrate how it integrates with the LLaMA 3.1 model. The use cases include: (1) Text Summarization, where LangChain condenses long texts into concise summaries; (2) Text Generation, which creatively produces narratives from prompts, exemplified by a whimsical story of a space-exploring cat; (3) Question Answering (QA), which extracts precise answers from contextual data; and (4) Data Extraction and Transformation, where unstructured text is converted into structured outputs like dates, names, and locations.

7: Agents – Granting LLMs Superpower: Introduces Agentic Technology as a transformative approach to building intelligent, goal-driven LLM applications by enabling autonomous task execution, dynamic reasoning, and integration with external tools. Using the LangChain framework, developers can integrate agents that execute tasks like web searches and mathematical calculations and use various other tools autonomously. Through a hands-on Python example, the chapter demonstrates how to build an agentic system that can, depending on the user input, call the appropriate tool to tell the current time by retrieving it from the environment or searching the internet for an answer to a user question. LLMs become significantly more dynamic, efficient, and useful for real-world applications by offloading specific tasks to agents.

8: Build LLM Application UI with Gradio: Demonstrates how to build user-friendly LLM application interfaces using Gradio. Inspired by the popularity of ChatGPT's conversational UI, the chapter highlights Gradio's strengths—rapid prototyping, session-aware interactions, and real-time streaming—making it ideal for LLM front-ends. Two applications are built: the first offers a simple prompt-response chat box that queries the LLM and returns static answers; the second extends functionality by maintaining conversation memory using LangChain and streaming the LLM's output for a more natural, ChatGPT-like experience.

9: Retrieval-Augmented Generation (RAG): This chapter introduces Retrieval-Augmented Generation (RAG) as a solution to the limitations of traditional LLMs, such as outdated knowledge, hallucinations, and lack of domain-specific expertise. The chapter demonstrates a practical RAG implementation using Chroma DB, a Vector Database, and LangChain, where users can upload PDFs (e.g., the 2025 Medicare Guide), ask questions, and receive streaming, contextually rich answers from the llama3.1 model. This setup enables interactive, domain-adaptive applications without retraining the model, showcasing the real-world value of RAG in building intelligent LLM-powered systems.

10: Evaluate Your LLM Application: This chapter focuses on building a practical evaluation pipeline for LLM applications, emphasizing that shipping without evaluation is risky since performance can drift due to changes in data, models, prompts, or infrastructure. It introduces two key evaluation approaches: creating a Python program that automates question/response evaluation using LLM-as-a-judge (where one LLM scores another's performance), and a more comprehensive program that benchmarks LLM performance across different platforms and CPU/GPU configurations.

11: Challenges and Future Trends with LLMs: Outlines key challenges and future trends of LLMs, including issues like data bias, hallucination, privacy, and environmental impact. Solutions such as RAG, model quantization, and sparse architectures aim to improve efficiency and accuracy. The rise of multimodal models expands AI capabilities beyond text, while the tension between open-source and proprietary approaches shapes innovation and accessibility. Looking ahead, LLMs will evolve into autonomous agents, personalized assistants, and energy-efficient systems, with increased focus on ethical governance and human-AI collaboration.

PART I: The Basics

1: How Large Language Models (LLMs) Work

Today, LLM technology is driving the field of Natural Language Processing (NLP). However, since the early days of computers, computer scientists have been trying to write software that could help computers interact with humans through natural language and speech. This natural language interaction differs from the most common means of human-computer interaction through the computer programming languages. Programming languages have limited vocabulary and follow strict programming rules and meanings; therefore, writing compiles that can convey the programmer's intent to the computer through strict programming language syntax is relatively easy. In contrast, human speech interaction with a computer is primarily unstructured, and the meaning conveyed is context sensitive. In addition, a typical human language vocabulary is large, and the exact words can combine different ways to mean different things. Hence, writing tools for natural language processing is complicated.

Early Attempts at NLP

ELIZA was one of the earliest natural language processing (NLP) programs, created in the mid-1960s by Joseph Weizenbaum at the MIT Artificial Intelligence Laboratory—the program simulated conversation using pattern matching and rule-based scripts rather than proper language understanding. It mimicked psychotherapists by reflecting user statements at them in a way that encouraged continued conversation. For example:

```
User: Hello, ELIZA.
ELIZA: How do you do? Please tell me your problem.
User: I am feeling sad today.
ELIZA: I am sorry to hear that you are feeling sad.
User: I don't think anyone understands me.
ELIZA: What makes you think that no one understands you?
User: People don't listen to me.
ELIZA: Do you believe that they should listen to you?
User: Yes, I do.
ELIZA: Why do you think you need their attention?
```

```
User: Because I feel lonely.
ELIZA: Tell me more about your loneliness.
User: I just don't have many friends.
ELIZA: Do you wish you had more friends?
User: Yes, I do.
ELIZA: What do you think prevents you from making more friends?
User: I guess I'm just too shy.
ELIZA: Do you often feel shy around others?
User: Yes, especially in large groups.
ELIZA: Why do you think large groups make you feel shy?
```

The responses from ELIZA were based on taking key phrases from the user and repeating them back to her, making ELIZA seem more intelligent than it actually was.

Rule-Based NLP Systems

In the nascent stages of NLP, systems were predominantly rule-based. These approaches depended on manually crafted rules and linguistic expertise to parse and interpret language. Key components of this era included:

- Phrase Structure Grammars: These define the syntactic structure of sentences by establishing fixed grammatical rules.
- Expert Systems: Specialized systems, such as early versions of machine translation engines like SYSTRAN, relied on a comprehensive set of hand-coded rules to perform language tasks.
- Finite-State Automata: Employed for pattern-matching tasks like spell-checking and simple text processing, these systems laid the groundwork for more complex NLP operations.

While these methods were effective within narrow domains, they lacked scalability and struggled with natural language's inherent ambiguity and variability.

Statistical Methods and Machine Learning Approaches

The limitations of rule-based systems spurred a shift towards statistical and machine learning methods as computational power increased, and large text datasets became available. This era witnessed several key innovations:

- N-grams: These probabilistic models predict the likelihood of a word based on its preceding words. Despite their simplicity, n-grams formed the backbone of early predictive text systems.
- Hidden Markov Models (HMMs): Widely used for tasks such as part-of-speech tagging and speech recognition, HMMs provide a framework for modeling sequential dependencies in language.
- Decision Trees and Support Vector Machines (SVMs): These algorithms advance text classification and sentiment analysis by enabling models to make decisions based on linguistic features.

Although these techniques significantly improved the performance of NLP systems, they often required extensive feature engineering. They were limited in their ability to capture the complex nuances of human language.

The Evolution of LLMs and Their Capabilities in NLP

The advent of deep learning marked a turning point in NLP. With the introduction of neural networks, particularly the Transformer architecture, NLP systems evolved into sophisticated Large Language Models (LLMs) that can process language with unprecedented depth and flexibility.

Transformer Architecture

The original transformer model consisted of an encoder-decoder structure. Encoders and decoders are explained later in the chapter. Although recent LLMs often use either the decoder (GPT-style) or the encoder (BERT-style).

Encoders

Encoders are responsible for understanding input text by transforming it into numerical representations (embeddings). Encoders work in the following way:

- Take an input sequence (e.g., a sentence).
- Break it up into words (tokens).
- Convert tokens into embeddings using a word/token embedding layer.
- Apply self-attention (explained later) and feedforward layers to capture contextual meaning.
- Output a contextualized representation of the input.

Decoders

Decoders are responsible for generating output text from a given input (such as a prompt or sequence). Decoders work in the following way:

- Receive some input context (e.g., from an encoder or previous decoder steps).
- Process the input using self-attention.
- Generate and predict the next word/token iteratively.

Encoder-Decoder (Seq2Seq) Architecture

Some models combine both encoders and decoders, where:

- The encoder processes the input text.
- The decoder generates the output.

Feature	Encoder (e.g., BERT)	Decoder (e.g., GPT)	Encoder-Decoder (e.g., T5)
Primary Function	Understand input	Generate output	Both
Self-Attention	Full bidirectional	Causal (left-to-right)	Both
Example Use Cases	Text classification, NER	Text generation, chatbots	Summarization, translation
Popular Models	BERT, RoBERTa	GPT-3, LLaMA	T5, BART

Table 1.1: Internal Architecture and the basic purpose of some popular LLMs.

Key takeaways from Table 1.1 above:

- Encoders are great for understanding language.
- Decoders are great for generating language.
- Encoder-Decoder models are powerful for sequence-to-sequence tasks like translation and summarization.

The other key innovation in transformers is the **self-attention mechanism,** which allows the model to weigh the importance of different words in a sentence regardless of their position. Unlike older models that process words sequentially, self-attention allows the model to look at all words in a sentence at once and determine their importance in relation to each other. For example, in the sentence: "The animal didn't cross the street because it was too tired." The word "it" could refer to "animal" or "street", but self-attention helps the model correctly assign importance and understand that "it" refers to "animal".

The self-attention enables more efficient parallelization than previous recurrent neural networks (RNNs) and long short-term memory (LSTM) networks, improving performance and scalability. To summarize, the key components of transformers are:

- Revolutionary Architecture: The paper proposed replacing traditional recurrent neural networks (RNNs) with a self-attention mechanism, allowing the model to weigh the importance of different words in a sentence simultaneously.
- Self-Attention Mechanism: This mechanism computes the relationships between all words in a sentence in parallel, significantly improving the efficiency and performance in handling long-range dependencies.
- Elimination of Recurrence: By discarding recurrence, Transformers enable more efficient training with parallel processing, which is particularly beneficial when working with large datasets (recurrence is the mechanism in RNNs where the network maintains a hidden state allowing the model to process sequential text or speech).
- Impact on Subsequent Research: The Transformer architecture has paved the way for subsequent models like BERT, GPT, and many others, dramatically advancing the state-of-the-art in various NLP tasks.
- Scalability and Performance: The design improves training speed and enhances the capability to capture complex language patterns, leading to more accurate and contextually aware language models.

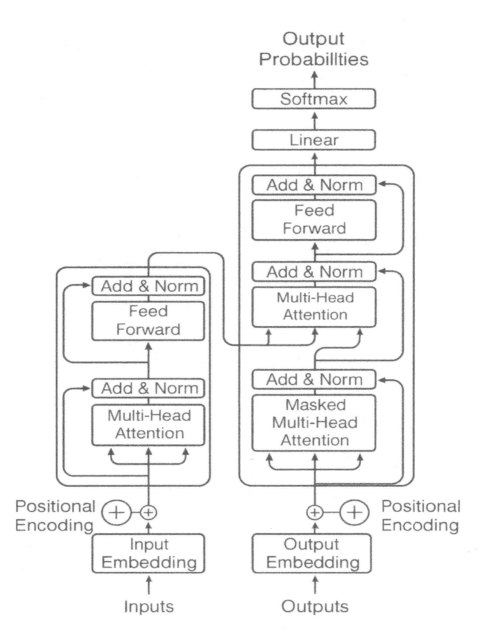

Figure 1.1: Building block of transformer architecture consisting of both encoder-decoder (Seq2Seq). This basic building block is repeated many times over for the complete LLM engine.

13

This diagram (Figure 1.1) illustrates the core architecture of a **Transformer** model, which forms the foundation for modern large language models (LLMs). It shows both the **encoder** (left) and **decoder** (right) stacks that together create a **sequence-to-sequence (Seq2Seq)** framework. Each encoder block consists of a **multi-head self-attention** mechanism followed by a **feed-forward neural network,** with residual connections and **layer normalization** after each sublayer. The input embeddings, combined with **positional encodings**, provide the encoder with information about the order of words in the sequence.

The decoder stack mirrors this structure but includes an additional **masked multi-head attention layer** at the bottom, ensuring that predictions for each token depend only on previously generated tokens (crucial for autoregressive generation). The decoder also includes an attention layer over the encoder outputs, allowing it to focus on relevant parts of the input sequence. Finally, the decoder output passes through a **linear layer** and a **softmax** function to generate probability distributions over the output vocabulary, producing the final predicted tokens. This repeated block design allows the model to efficiently capture long-range dependencies and complex linguistic patterns.

Training Process for the LLM: Pre-Training and Fine-Tuning Approaches

Pre-Training

LLMs undergo an extensive pre-training phase using massive datasets scraped from the internet, books, research papers, and other text sources. The product of this pre-training is a base model, also called a foundation model. During this phase, the model learns to predict missing words, complete sentences, and understand language structure using objectives such as:

- Masked Language Modeling (MLM): Used in models like BERT, where certain words are masked, and the model predicts them.
- Causal Language Modeling (CLM): Used in GPT models, where the model predicts the next word in a sequence given the previous word.
- Next Sentence Prediction (NSP): Helps the model learn contextual relationships between sentences.

At a high level, pre-training a blank LLM is straightforward. The first step is to create a Neural Network with many layers using the Pytorch software package (torch). Initially, this network model, the blank LLM, has all its internal weights set randomly. Second, a massive corpus of text data is gathered to train this neural network. The raw text data is first pre-processed (tokenized - split into words or sub-words) and turned into numbers to feed the stream of numbers into the LLM as input. This pre-processing is called embedding the raw text.

Note that no data labeling is done on the input text. So, how does the training process proceed and then complete without any labeled input? The answer is that since, at this stage, the model is only being trained to predict the next word in a sentence, part of the input text is hidden from the LLM, and it is hidden part(s) that the model tries to guess.

The training process successively moves the hidden word(s) window until the whole sentence, minus the last word, is fed to the LLM. The internal model weights are adjusted depending on how successful or not the LLM is in predicting the next word. This process is repeated thousands of times with millions of sentences until the LLM can predict the next word in a random input sentence with some success. Note that the knowledge the LLM learned by seeing millions of sentences is captured in the billions of internal parameter values (weights) adjusted during the training process.

Due to the amount of data fed through the LLM and the computation complexity needed to adjust the parameter weights properly, developing a pre-trained foundation model requires tremendous hardware resources, including costly GPUs, and often months. Since this book is about LLMs running on workstations, and training them on a workstation is impractical, pre-training an LLM is not discussed.

At the end of this pre-training, the base LLM can carry out generalized language tasks like sentence completion. Additional fine-tuning training is required for the model to do specialized tasks like question-answers (like a chatbot) or provide answers to domain-specific questions.

Fine-Tuning

After pre-training, base LLMs can be fine-tuned on specific datasets to optimize their performance for particular applications. Fine-tuning involves further training on domain-specific text or task-oriented data. For this step, a large amount of labeled and curated data is again fed into the model; however, the amount of data will be in the range of thousands of embedded tokens, not millions, like for the pre-training step. This is still a resource-intensive and time-consuming step, so several optimized methods have been devised to cut down computation, memory, and time requirements to fine-tune an LLM. Methods include:

- Supervised Fine-Tuning: Using labeled datasets to improve model accuracy on targeted tasks.
- Reinforcement Learning from Human Feedback (RLHF): A technique where human evaluators help refine model outputs to align with desired behavior.
- Parameter-Efficient Fine-Tuning (PEFT): Methods like LoRA (Low-Rank Adaptation) that modify only small portions of the model to reduce computational costs.

Again, since this book is about how to use LLMs running on local workstations, and to properly fine-tune a base model still requires extensive computing, GPU, and labeled data resources far beyond what is available on a workstation, this book does not deal with the fine-tuning process. Instead, we focus on a technique called Retrieval Augmented Generation (RAG) to customize a base model, the llama 3.1, to answer questions only from the information available from the documents for a specific purpose (Chapter 9).

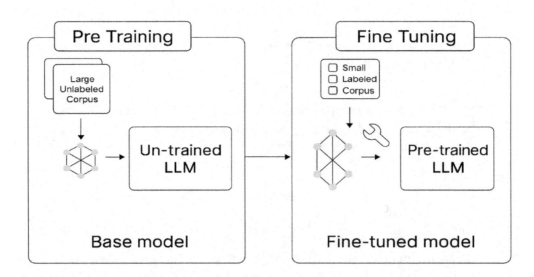

Figure 1.2: The steps of training an un-trained LLM to a pre-trained base model with a vast quantity of unlabeled data and then further fine-tuning the

model for specific tasks like chat, question-answering, or reasoning with a smaller set of labeled data.

The Role of Large-Scale Datasets

The effectiveness of LLMs heavily depends on the size and quality of training datasets (also called corpus). These corpora are curated from:

- Public Web Data: Wikipedia, Common Crawl, books, and research papers.
- Code Repositories: GitHub, Stack Overflow for coding-related tasks
- Conversational Data: Dialogue datasets from social media and chat interactions.
- Scientific and Academic Papers: arXiv, PubMed for specialized knowledge.

For example, the training dataset for GPT-3 was composed of a mixture of publicly available and licensed datasets. OpenAI has provided some details about the sources and their sizes (in tokens), though not all specifics are fully disclosed. Table 1.2 below shows the breakdown of the sources and approximate sizes of the GPT-3 training data:

Dataset Source	Approximate Size (in Tokens)	Description
Common Crawl	410B	A large-scale web dataset collected over several years, filtered and processed for high-quality content.
WebText2	19B	A refined dataset based on OpenAI's WebText (used for GPT-2), consisting of high-quality web pages such as discussions and articles.
Books1 & Books2	67B	Two undisclosed book datasets that include fiction and non-fiction texts.
Wikipedia	3B	A snapshot of English Wikipedia (filtered for quality).
Other Internet Data	47B	Various sources, likely including news articles, forums, and other high-quality web content.

Table 1.2: Sources & Sizes of GPT-3 Training Data. Total Dataset Size: ~570 billion tokens. Note the following: 1 token is approximately 4 characters of English text. The dataset was carefully filtered to remove low-quality content and duplication. While OpenAI provided these details in their GPT-3 paper, they have not fully disclosed all sources due to licensing and proprietary reasons.

Comparison of major LLMs

Feature	GPT-4 (OpenAI)	Gemini 1 (Google)	Claude 2 (Anthropic)	LLaMA 2 (Meta)
Model Type	Decoder-only Transformer	Decoder-only Transformer	Decoder-only Transformer	Decoder-only Transformer
Training Data	Public & proprietary	Public & proprietary	Public & proprietary	Public & proprietary
Fine-Tuning	RLHF	RLHF	RLHF	RLHF
Multimodal Support	Yes (text, images)	Yes (text, images)	No	No
Context Length	~128K tokens	~1M tokens	~100K tokens	~65K tokens
Best For	General knowledge, coding, chatbots	Multimodal applications, search	Safety-focused applications, ethics-driven AI	Open-source applications, research

Table 1.3: This comparison highlights the distinct capabilities of major LLMs. Google, Meta, and Anthropic lead in AI innovation; their models cater to different use cases based on their architecture, training data, and fine-tuning methodologies.

2: Install and Configure the Ollama Software on Your Workstation

Overview of Ollama

Ollama is a lightweight, efficient, yet very powerful framework for running Large Language Models (LLMs) locally on a personal workstation. It provides a simple interface to manage, run, and interact with models like LLaMA, Mistral, and others.

Why Run an LLM Locally with Ollama?

Unlike cloud-based LLM services, running an LLM locally with Ollama offers several benefits:

- Privacy & Security: Local execution ensures sensitive data never leaves your machine.
- No API Limits or Costs: Avoid recurring costs and API rate limits associated with cloud-based LLMs.
- Customization: Modify and fine-tune models as needed.
- Offline Accessibility: Use LLM capabilities without requiring an internet connection.
- Reduced Latency: Running models on a local machine eliminates network-induced delays.

Installing Ollama on Ubuntu

The best way to get started with Ollama software is to head to the **ollama.com** website (or **ollama.ai**).

Figure 2.1: Ollama.com home page.

Click on the Download button in the middle of the page, and the system should detect and take you to the correct download area for your platform. In our case, our workstation is running Ubuntu release 24.04, and the Linux page is shown with one command installation script.

Figure 2.2: One line download and installation script from ollama.com home page.

Copy and run the command from the Ollama website from a terminal on your workstation. This command will install the latest version of the ollama software, or upgrade to the newest version, if ollama is already installed on the system. The installer will also detect if a GPU is installed on the system.

It is recommended that the system packages be updated before installing Ollma. Use the command below to update the System Packages.

```
$ sudo apt update && sudo apt upgrade -y
```

Now run the one-line installer command shown below:

```
$ curl -fsSL https://ollama.com/install.sh | sh
$ curl -fsSL https://ollama.com/install.sh | sh
>>> Installing ollama to /usr/local
>>> Downloading Linux amd64 bundle
#################################################### 100.0%
>>> Adding ollama user to render group...
>>> Adding ollama user to video group...
>>> Adding current user to ollama group...
>>> Creating ollama systemd service...
>>> Enabling and starting ollama service...
>>> NVIDIA GPU installed.
```

To check if Ollama is installed correctly, run:

```
$ ollama --version
ollama version is 0.11.10
```

If the installation was successful, it will return the installed Ollama version. Then type:

```
$ ollama list
NAME              ID             SIZE      MODIFIED
llama3.1:latest   46e0c10c039e   4.9 GB    3 weeks ago
```

The **list** command above shows download models; the list will be empty if no models have been downloaded yet. By following these steps, you will have Ollama installed on your workstation and will be able to interact with the llama 3.1 LLM locally.

Visiting the ollma repository

To download and use a model from the Ollama repository, visit Ollama website URL: **https://ollama.com/**and go to the list of the available models by selecting **Models** from the top left menu. Here is a partial list of some of the powerful LLMs freely available for download to your local workstation. Newer and more powerful models are being added all the time.

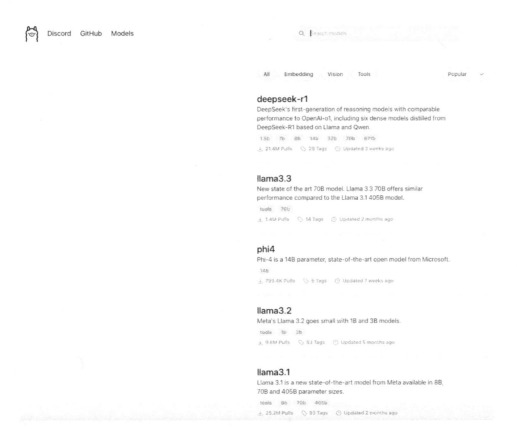

Figure 2.1: List and description of free downloadable models available from the Ollama website.

This book will use the llama3.1 LLM to experiment with our Python code. Not all models available in the repository will fit in your local workstation; our own workstation has 32GB of RAM, and a GPU with 11GB of memory, so we chose the 7 billion parameter llama 3.1 LLM from Meta to work with. The 14 billion parameter phi4 LLM form Microsoft also worked well, but models larger than that, like some 70 billion parameter models, will not fit.

To pull the llama3.1 Model from Repository

Type on the terminal:

```
$ ollama pull llama3.1
```

This command downloads the latest version of the llama 3.1 model and stores in the local workstation in the **/usr/share/ollama/.ollama/models** directory (for the Ubuntu OS).

Running Ollama in Chat Mode

One of the key features of the Ollama server is its ability to run in an interactive chat mode right out of the box. In this mode:

- The server maintains contextual memory, allowing it to track ongoing conversations.
- User input is continuously processed, and responses are generated based on previous exchanges.

To run the model, type the command below. If the model was not downloaded earlier with a pull command, the run command will also download the model and launch an interactive chat session prompt (>>>) where you can ask questions.

```
$ ollama run llama3.1
```

```
>>> What is the capital of France?
```

```
The capital of France is Paris.

>>> Send a message (/? for help)

>>> /bye
```

The run command can also be executed with –verbose option that will display
various performance matrices from the ollama/LLM combination.

```
$ ollama run llama3.1 –verbose

>>> hi

How's it going? Is there something I can help you with or would you
like to chat?


total duration:        770.932592ms

load duration:         193.525787ms

prompt eval count:     11 token(s)

prompt eval duration: 107.700951ms

prompt eval rate:      102.13 tokens/s

eval count:            21 token(s)

eval duration:         469.122172ms

eval rate:             44.76 tokens/s

>>> Send a message (/? for help
```

Metric	Value	Units	Explanation
Total duration	770.932592	ms	End-to-end server-side time for the turn (≈ load + prompt eval + eval + small overhead).
Load duration	193.525787	ms	Time to load/prepare the model (map weights, init tokenizer, build caches).
Prompt eval count	11	tokens	Number of input tokens consumed (your text + system/template/special tokens).
Prompt eval duration	107.700951	ms	Time to prefill/evaluate the input tokens before any output appears (impacts TTFT).

Prompt eval rate	102.13	tokens/s	Throughput during prefill (input tokens processed per second).
Eval count	21	tokens	Number of output tokens generated by the model for this reply.
Eval duration	469.122172	ms	Time spent generating the output tokens (streaming "typing" phase).
Eval rate	44.76	tokens/s	Throughput during generation (output tokens produced per second).

Some essential Ollama CLI commands:

Command	Description
ollma --version	Displays ollama version
ollama list	Lists all installed models.
ollama pull <model>	Downloads a specified model from the registry.
ollama run <model>	Runs an instance of the specified model interactively.
ollama serve	Starts an API server to interact with models.
ollama stop	Stops a running instance of a model.
ollama rm <model>	Uninstalls a specific model from the system.
ollama create <model>	Creates a custom model using a modelfile.
ollama help	Displays the help menu with a list of available commands.
ollama show <model>	Creates a custom model using a modelfile.

Table 2.1: Ollama CLI Commands

Understanding the Ollama Framework - What is Going on Under the Hood

The Ollama framework provides a flexible environment for running large language models locally through chat mode (as we did in the previous section to test the Ollama installation process), HTTP endpoints, or Python integration.

26

Understanding server management operations to model management allows developers to leverage their capabilities efficiently. Additionally, the ability to compile Ollama software from the source offers advanced users the ability to customize it. By mastering these aspects, developers can harness the full potential of Ollama in their applications.

How the Ollama Server Runs in the Background

When you install and run Ollama software, it operates a background server process that manages model execution and interactions. The Ollama server is designed to be lightweight and efficient, acting as a bridge between the user and the AI model. It performs several critical functions:

- Model Management: The server maintains a repository of downloaded models, ensuring they are readily available for execution.
- Memory and Execution Handling: It optimizes memory allocation and GPU/CPU usage to efficiently run large models.
- Task Queueing: The server handles multiple concurrent requests and queues tasks as necessary to ensure smooth operation.

The Ollama server typically starts as a background process upon system boot or manual execution, allowing seamless access to models without requiring repeated initialization. Command showing Ollama service running in the Background:

```
$ systemctl status ollama.service
```

● ollama.service - ollama Service

    Loaded: loaded (/etc/systemd/system/ollama.service; enabled; preset: enabled)

    Active: active (running) since Wed 2025-02-12 11:44:01 EST; 2 weeks 1 day ago

  Main PID: 1722 (ollama)

    Tasks: 15 (limit: 38058)

    Memory: 4.8G (peak: 9.5G)

      CPU: 4min 34.529s

```
CGroup: /system.slice/ollama.service
       └─1722 /usr/local/bin/ollama serve
```

How the Ollama Server Interfaces with Downloaded Models

Ollama server provides an intuitive mechanism to manage and interact with the LLMs. Upon downloading a model, the server:

- Stores the Model Locally: The downloaded model files are saved in a designated directory, typically within /usr/share/ollama/.ollama/models.
- Loads the Model into Memory: When a request is made, the server dynamically loads the model into RAM, optimizing performance for subsequent queries.
- Executes Inference Requests: The server communicates with the underlying model engine (such as Llama or GPT-based architectures) to process input and generate responses.
- Caches Results for Optimization: Ollama may cache responses and leverage efficient execution techniques to reduce redundant computation.

As we saw in the earlier section, the Ollama server can run in chat mode, similar to how most of us use ChatGPT.

```
$ ollama run <model-name>
```

The run command starts an interactive session with the named model in the background. It presents the user with an interactive chat session prompt (>>>) where she can input queries and receive responses from the requested model.

Connection to the llama3.1 LLM being served by Ollama server via an HTTP Endpoint

The Ollama server can also be exposed as an HTTP service, allowing external applications to interface via RESTful API calls. This method of interfacing is particularly useful for integrating AI capabilities into web applications, chatbots, and other services. If not already started, start the Ollama server as before:

```
$ ollama run llama3.1
```

Once running, http clients like curl, and postman can send HTTP POST requests to interact with the model. A typical request structure looks like this:

```
$ curl -X POST -H "Content-Type: application/json" -d '{"model":
"llama3.1", "prompt": "What is the capital of  France?"}'
```

```
{"model":"llama3.1","created_at":"2025-02-
28T22:50:27.296503244Z","response":"The","done":false}

{"model":"llama3.1","created_at":"2025-02-
28T22:50:27.323016168Z","response":" capital","done":false}

{"model":"llama3.1","created_at":"2025-02-
28T22:50:27.347689396Z","response":" of","done":false}

{"model":"llama3.1","created_at":"2025-02-
28T22:50:27.371439077Z","response":" France","done":false}

{"model":"llama3.1","created_at":"2025-02-
28T22:50:27.394832494Z","response":" is","done":false}

{"model":"llama3.1","created_at":"2025-02-
28T22:50:27.418177819Z","response":" Paris","done":false}

{"model":"llama3.1","created_at":"2025-02-
28T22:50:27.441439108Z","response":".","done":false}

{"model":"llama3.1","created_at":"2025-02-
28T22:50:27.464769499Z","response":"","done":true,"done_reason":"sto
p","context":[128006,882,128007,271,3923,374,279,6864,315,9822,30,12
8009,128006,78191,128007,271,791,6864,315,9822,374,12366,13],"total_
duration":2570005234,"load_duration":2292002516,"prompt_eval_count":
17,"prompt_eval_duration":104000000,"eval_count":8,"eval_duration":1
73000000}
```

The response contains the token-by-token AI-generated response text (with additional meta-data). In this example, the LLM is operating in a streaming mode.

A very useful command is:

```
$ ollama show llama3.1
  Model
    architecture        llama
    parameters          8.0B
    context length      131072
```

```
    embedding length    4096
    quantization        Q4_K_M


  Capabilities
    completion
    tools


  Parameters
    stop    "<|start_header_id|>"
    stop    "<|end_header_id|>"
    stop    "<|eot_id|>"


  License
    LLAMA 3.1 COMMUNITY LICENSE AGREEMENT
    Llama 3.1 Version Release Date: July 23, 2024
    ...
```

The **ollama show** command displays various internal parameter settings for the model. The llama3.1 model we are using has 8 billion parameters, and has a context length of 128K (131072/1024 - more about this critical parameter later).

Testing a model other than llama3.1 with a different Ollama command

Although we primarily use the llama3.1 model in this book, we will download and use a different model and demonstrate another way of invoking the Ollama server in this section.

Here, we create a file (called modelfile) with instructions on creating a customized LLM based on the mistral model from the Ollama repository. In this file, we also direct the LLM using system prompts (see Chapter 4) to instruct it as to what it will be used for.

```
$ cat modelfile
```

```
# use the mistral model

FROM mistral

# set the system prompt

SYSTEM "You are travel expert."
```

Then the create command is used to create a customized LLM called capital.
The create command first downloads the mistral model and then creates the
new capital model from it.

```
$ ollama create capital -f ./modelfile

gathering model components

pulling manifest

pulling ff82381e2bea... 100%

   4.1 GB

pulling ed11eda7790d... 100%

      30 B

pulling 42347cd80dc8... 100%

     485 B

verifying sha256 digest

writing manifest

success

using existing layer
sha256:ff82381e2bea77d91c1b824c7afb83f6fb73e9f7de9dda631bcdbca564aa5
435

creating new layer
sha256:023126895d350afc57310c5c6505948312b2a449679d4abe07f96b49c8837
871

using existing layer
sha256:ed11eda7790d05b49395598a42b155812b17e263214292f7b87d15e14003d
337

writing manifest

success
```

```
$ ollama list
NAME              ID             SIZE      MODIFIED
capital:latest    19b805855ea8   4.1 GB    45 minutes ago
mistral:latest    f974a74358d6   4.1 GB    45 minutes ago
llama3.1:latest   46e0c10c039e   4.9 GB    5 weeks ago
```

The new model called capital can be invoked with the following command in chat mode:

```
$ ollama run capital
```

```
>>> who are you?

 I am a travel assistant, designed to help answer questions about
various destinations, provide suggestions for activities, offer tips
on planning trips, and share interesting travel-related facts! I
don't

have personal experiences or emotions, but I strive to be as helpful
and informative as possible in the realm of travel. Let me know if
you have any specific questions or need assistance with your next

adventure!


>>> Send a message (/? for help)
```

Setting up concurrency in Ollama server

By default, the Ollama server runs in a single-threaded, single-model mode. This mode of operation restricts the user to asking one question to one loaded LLM model at a time. When the following commands are run from two different terminals:

From Terminal 1:

```
$ ollama run phi3:latest
```

```
>>> Can you explain in detail why the ocean is blue?
```

Form terminal 2:

```
$ ollama run deepseek-r1:1.5b
```

```
>>> Can you explain in detail why the sky is blue?
```

Suppose the **Enter** key is pressed simultaneously in both terminals. The terminal that registers the keypress first will load the model and start answering the question. The other terminal will wait for the first question to be answered, unload the loaded model, load the new model, and proceed to answer the question in the second terminal. This severe restriction can be removed by configuring two environment variables used by the ollama server. These are (note the uppercase):

OLLAMA_NUM_PARALLEL

OLLAMA_MAX_LOADED_MODELS

In our setup, since the Ollama server is configured to run as a system service called ollama.service, the service has to be configured to take advantage of the concurrency environment properties.

First, modify the ollama.service by taking the following steps:

```
$ sudo EDITOR=vi systemctl edit ollama.service
```

Then, add the line below to the configuration file, save it, and restart the service.

Editing /etc/systemd/system/ollama.service.d/override.conf

Anything between here and the comment below will become the contents of the drop-in file

[Service]

Environment="OLLAMA_NUM_PARALLEL=2" "OLLAMA_MAX_LOADED_MODELS=2"

Edits below this comment will be discarded

```
$ sudo systemctl daemon-reload

$ sudo systemctl restart ollama.service

$ sudo systemctl status ollama.service
```

Once the ollama.service restarts, set up the two terminals with two different LLMs, and ask two different questions as before. This time, both terminals will simultaneously start outputting the answers without pausing for the first terminal to complete its response to the question.

You can also verify that two models are loaded in the memory:

```
$ ollama ps
```

NAME	ID	SIZE	PROCESSOR	CONTEXT
UNTIL				
phi3:latest	4f2222927938	6.5 GB	100%	
GPU 4096	4 minutes from now			
deepseek-r1:1.5b	e0979632db5a	2.0 GB	100%	
GPU 4096	4 minutes from now			

The only caveat is that the GPU must have enough VRAM to load both models simultaneously.

Downloading and Compiling Ollama from GitHub

For those who want to explore the internals of Ollama software further or contribute to its development, the Ollama software can be downloaded and compiled from its GitHub repository.

Cloning the Repository

To get started, clone the official repository:

```
$ git clone https://github.com/ollama/ollama.git
```

Installing Dependencies

Before building Ollama, ensure you have the necessary dependencies installed. This may include:

- Go programming language
- NVIDIA CUDA library (if using GPU acceleration)

Building Ollama

Once dependencies are installed, build the Ollama project using the command:

```
$ go build -o ollama ./cmd/ollama
```

This compiles the Ollama executable, which can then be used to run models locally. After compiling, start the Ollama server:

```
$ ./ollama serve
```

This will launch the background process, allowing interaction with AI models just like the prebuilt Ollama software binaries.

3: First LLM Applications with Python

This chapter will guide you through setting up and running a Python application that interacts with an LLM to answer simple queries, such as "What is the capital of France?". We will use the llama3.1 model served by an Ollama server running in the background.

Prerequisites

Before proceeding, ensure you have the following dependencies installed on your system:

- Python 3.10+
- Ollama server (installed and running in the background)
- Necessary Python libraries
- Optionally, NVIDIA GPU and CUDA libraries installed for performance.

Run Ollama and Load llama3.1

Once Ollama is installed, start the Ollama server and pull the required model:

```
$ ollama pull llama3.1
```

Verify that a suitable LLM is available locally.

```
$ ollama list
```

NAME	ID	SIZE	MODIFIED
llama3.1:latest	46e0c10c039e	4.9 GB	3 weeks ago

This should display llama3.1 as an available model (downloaded by the pull command above).

Calling the Ollama Server from Python Code

In addition to providing the user the ability to interact with the LLM of choice from the Ollama CLI, Ollama also provides a convenient way to be invoke LLMs from Python scripts. This allows developers to integrate AI models into their applications without dealing with complex server setups. Start by install some of the needed Python modules.

```
$ pip install requests
```

A Python program can interact with the Ollama server using HTTP requests, as shown below:

```
$ cat chapter3-1.py
```

```python
# Import required libraries
import requests  # To handle HTTP requests to the Ollama
server

# Define the base URL of the locally running Ollama API server
OLLAMA_API_URL = "http://localhost:11434/api/generate"

# Define the user input prompt (question we want to ask the
LLM)
prompt = "What is the capital of France?"

# Prepare the data (payload) that will be sent in the POST
request to the server
payload = {
    "model": "llama3.1",  # Specify which model to use (in
this case, Llama 3.1)
    "prompt": prompt,      # The question or instruction for
the model
    "stream": False        # Whether to receive a streaming
response or a full response at once
}
# Send the POST request to the Ollama server with the payload
as JSON
response = requests.post(OLLAMA_API_URL, json=payload)

# Check if the request was successful (HTTP status code 200
means OK)
if response.status_code == 200:
    # Parse the JSON response body
    result = response.json()
```

```
    # Print out the model's answer from the 'response' field
    print("Response:", result["response"])
else:
    # If the request failed, print out the error code and
error message
    print("Error:", response.status_code, response.text)
```

Now run the program

```
$ python3 chapter3-1.py
```

Response: The capital of France is Paris.

The Ollama Python module

The Ollama Python module provides several functions to interact with models
hosted on an Ollama server. The official Ollama Python library is hosted on
GitHub, providing comprehensive information on installation, usage, and
examples (https://github.com/ollama/ollama-python).

Function	Description
ollama.chat()	Chat-based interaction with history
ollama.generate()	Simple text generation (completion)
ollama.pull()	Downloads a model
ollama.create()	Creates a custom model from a modelfile
ollama.list()	Lists locally available models
ollama.run()	Runs a model with a prompt (alternative to generate())
ollama.delete()	Deletes a model
ollama.show()	Shows model metadata
ollama.embeddings()	Generates embeddings from text

Table 3.1: Summary of Ollama API calls

We can also install a Python module to facilitate more direct interaction with the LLM without using the Ollama server URL.

```
$ pip install ollama
```

```
$ cat chapter3-2.py
```

```python
# Import the ollama library
# This library allows us to interact with a local Ollama
server to query language models like Llama 3.1
import ollama

# Define a function to query the Ollama server with a user
prompt
def query_ollama(prompt, model="llama3.1"):
    """
    Sends a prompt to the specified Ollama model and returns
the response.

    Args:
        prompt (str): The user's input/question to send to the
model.
        model (str): The model to query (default is
'llama3.1').

    Returns:
        dict: The full response from the Ollama server,
including the model's output.
    """
    # Call the Ollama server's chat function
    # 'model' specifies which language model to use
    # 'messages' contains a list of conversational turns (in
this case, a single user message)
    response = ollama.chat(
        model=model,
        messages=[{"role": "user", "content": prompt}]  #
Format: Role (user), Content (the prompt text)
    )

    # Return the entire server response (a dictionary
containing model's answer and other metadata)
    return response

# Test the function by asking "What is the capital of France?"
# The output will be the model's response in a dictionary
format
print(query_ollama("What is the capital of France?"))
```

Now run the program

```
$ python3 chapter3-2.py

model='llama3.1' created_at='2025-02-28T21:36:35.983293137Z'
done=True done_reason='stop' total_duration=2575992235
load_duration=2290531992 prompt_eval_count=17
prompt_eval_duration=101000000 eval_count=8 eval_duration=182000000
message=Message(role='assistant', content='The capital of France is
Paris.', images=None, tool_calls=None)
```

The two Python programs above show two different ways of interacting with
the llama3.1 model and the Ollama server. First, accessing the Ollama server
using HTTP is useful when the model is running on a separate model server
from the machine where the application is running. The second method is
directly accessing the model using the Ollama Python library, which is more
appropriate if both the application and the model server are on the same
machine.

Setting up the Python environment and various dependencies needed to run the Python code in the book

We highly recommend creating a Python virtual environment (venv) to run the
book's Python code. Venv creates an isolated workspace for Python projects. It
prevents conflicts between dependencies of different projects and helps manage
Python packages efficiently.

How to Set Up a Python Virtual Environment in Ubuntu

Install Python and venv (if not installed).

```
$ sudo apt update
```

```
$ sudo apt install python3 python3-venv python3-pip -y
```

Navigate to your project directory and run:

```
$ python3 -m venv .venv
```

This creates a virtual environment named .venv, which will be automatically
recognized by popular Python IDE like VS CODE. To activate the virtual
environment manually, run the following:

```
$ source    .venv/bin/activate
```

To install Packages Inside the Virtual Environment:

```
(.venv)$ pip install requests
```

Deactivate the Virtual Environment :

```
(.venv)$ deactivate
```

To verify the NVIDIA GPU and CUDA library is available on your Ubuntu workstation:

```
$ nvidia-smi
```

```
Sat Mar  1 14:12:36 2025

+-----------------------------------------------------------------------------
| NVIDIA-SMI 550.120            Driver Version: 550.120      CUDA Version: 12.4
|
|-----------------------------------+----------------------+-------------------
| GPU  Name                Persistence-M | Bus-Id        Disp.A | Volatile Uncorr. ECC
|
| Fan  Temp   Perf         Pwr:Usage/Cap |         Memory-Usage | GPU-Util  Compute M.
|
|                                   |                      |               MIG M.
|
|===================================+======================+===================
|   0  NVIDIA GeForce GTX 1080 Ti    Off |  00000000:01:00.0  On |               N/A
|
| 25%   34C    P8          17W / 250W |    548MiB / 11264MiB |    19%      Default
|
|                                   |                      |               N/A
|
+-----------------------------------+----------------------+-------------------


+-----------------------------------------------------------------------------
| Processes:
|
|  GPU   GI   CI        PID   Type   Process name                      GPU Memory
|
|        ID   ID                                                       Usage
|
|=============================================================================
|    0   N/A  N/A      2310      G   /usr/lib/xorg/Xorg                     333MiB
|
|    0   N/A  N/A      2598      G   /usr/bin/gnome-shell                    48MiB
|
|    0   N/A  N/A      3168      G   /usr/libexec/xdg-desktop-portal-gnome   18MiB
|
|    0   N/A  N/A      6411      G   ...seed-version=20250211-180335.527000  104MiB
|
|    0   N/A  N/A     82524      G   ...erProcess --variations-seed-version   36MiB
|
+-----------------------------------------------------------------------------
```

PART II: The Core

4: Prompting and LLM Context

Prompting is crucial in interacting with Large Language Models (LLMs) because it directly influences the quality, relevance, and accuracy of the model's responses. A well-structured unambiguous prompt provides clear instructions to the LLM, guiding the model toward producing more useful and context-aware outputs. Effective prompting can enhance reasoning, creativity, and problem-solving by shaping the way the LLM interprets and processes information.

What is "Prompting"?

One of the impressive abilities of a Generative Pre-trained Transformer (GPT) model is its ability to generate human-like text when interacting with the user. The most common way for this human LLM interaction is via Chat Interface, where the user "prompts" the GPT model for a response. The GPT response's quality and usefulness depend significantly on the preciseness of the prompts provided by this user during the interaction with the LLM.

Since LLMs do not "think" like humans but rather generate text based on probability distributions learned from vast amounts of training data, well-structured prompts are essential to achieving accurate and relevant responses. At its core, prompting is an interface between the user and the LLM. It allows users to convey instructions, ask questions, or define constraints that shape the model's output. The effectiveness of an LLM largely depends on how well it is prompted. By employing techniques such as clarity, role-based prompting, and chain-of-thought reasoning, users can maximize the potential of LLMs.

Basic Techniques for Creating Good Prompts:

	Description	Example Prompts
Simple and Direct Prompting	Ask straightforward questions or give clear tasks.	Explain the concept of recursion in programming. List five famous painters from the Renaissance period. Describe the lifecycle of a butterfly.
Role-Based Prompting	Assign a role or expertise to guide style and depth of response.	Act as a professional software engineer and explain the advantages of using Python for data science. You are a nutritionist. Recommend a healthy weekly meal plan for a vegetarian. Imagine you are a travel guide. Describe a one-day itinerary for visiting Paris.
Zero-Shot Prompting	Ask the model to perform a task without examples—just based on instruction.	Summarize the key points of the Declaration of Independence. Translate the sentence 'Good morning, how are you?' into French. Write a haiku about winter. Explain the difference between machine learning and deep learning in simple terms.
Few-Shot Prompting	Provide a few examples to show the expected pattern.	Convert sentences into passive voice: The cat chased the mouse. $\rightarrow$ The mouse was chased by the cat. She wrote a letter. $\rightarrow$ A letter was written by her. He repaired the bicycle. $\rightarrow$ The bicycle was repaired by him. The chef cooked a delicious meal. $\rightarrow$ A delicious meal was cooked by the chef.

Chain-of-Thought Prompting	Encourage reasoning step-by-step before final answer.	Solve the following math problem and explain each step: A train travels at 60 mph for 2 hours and then 40 mph for 3 hours. What is the total distance covered? Find the prime factors of 84. Show all calculations step-by-step. Explain how photosynthesis works, describing each stage in order.
Instruction-Based Prompting	Give clear structured instructions for output.	Write a Python function that checks whether a given number is a prime number. Include comments explaining each step. Create a bullet-point summary of the causes of World War I. Draft a professional email requesting a meeting with a client.

Table 3.1: Examples of prompt types.

Effective prompting techniques can significantly enhance an LLM's output. Note that Few-shot prompting examples help the model learn the pattern you expect. Chain-of-thought prompting improves reasoning in complex tasks. Zero-shot prompting depends purely on how explicit your instruction is.

Command-Line Prompt Interaction with llama 3.1

You can interact with llama3.1 LLM via the command line in Chat mode.

```
$ ollama run llama3.1
```

```
>>> what is the capital of UK?
```

```
The United Kingdom (UK) is a sovereign state that consists of four
constituent countries: England,

Scotland, Wales, and Northern Ireland.

Each country has its own capital city:

* The capital of **England** is London.

* The capital of **Scotland** is Edinburgh.

* The capital of **Wales** is Cardiff.

* The capital of **Northern Ireland** is Belfast.

So, it depends on which part of the UK you're referring to!

>>> can you only provide the capital of england?

The capital of England is:

London

>>> can you provide the answer in CAPS?

THE CAPITAL OF ENGLAND IS:

LONDON

>>> just provide the name of the capital in caps

LONDON

>>> /bye
```

By using well-crafted prompts, you can direct the LLM to provide the most
relevant answers.

Using Python code to prompt llama3.1 LLM

Below is Python code that interactively sends a prompt from the user to the
llama 3.1 model running in the background.

```
$ cat  chapter4.1.py
```

```
# Import required libraries
```

```python
import requests  # For sending HTTP requests to the Ollama
server

# Define the URL endpoint for the local Ollama server's
generate API
OLLAMA_API_URL = "http://localhost:11434/api/generate"

# Print welcome message to the user
print("Interactive Llama 3.1 Chatbot")
print("Type 'q' to exit.\n")  # Provide instructions on how to
exit

# Start an infinite loop to allow continuous interaction with
the chatbot
while True:
    # Prompt the user for input
    prompt = input("You: ")

    # Check if the user wants to quit
    if prompt.lower() == 'q':
        print("Exiting...")  # Notify that the program is
exiting
        break  # Break the loop to end the program

    # Prepare the payload (data) to send in the HTTP POST
request
    payload = {
        "model": "llama3.1",  # Specify the model name to use
        "prompt": prompt,     # Pass the user's message as the
prompt
        "stream": False       # Set to False to receive a full
response (not streamed in parts)
    }

    try:
        # Send the POST request to the Ollama server with the
payload formatted as JSON
        response = requests.post(OLLAMA_API_URL, json=payload)

        # Check if the request was successful
        if response.status_code == 200:
            # If successful, parse the JSON response
            result = response.json()
            # Display the model's response to the user
            print("Llama 3.1:", result.get("response", "No
response received."))
        else:
            # If the server returns an error status, display
the error code and message
```

```
        print("Error:", response.status_code,
response.text)

    except requests.exceptions.RequestException as e:
        # Handle exceptions such as server connection errors
        print("Error connecting to Ollama server:", e)
```

Now run the program:

```
$ python3 chapter4.1.py
```

```
python3 chapter4-1.py

Interactive Llama 3.1 Chatbot

Type 'q' to exit.


You: what is the capital of france?

Llama 3.1: The capital of France is Paris.

You: and england?

Llama 3.1: It seems like you started to ask a question, but it got
cut off! You mentioned "and England"? Could you please complete your
question so I can provide a helpful response? Are you asking about
something related to England or comparing it with another country?

You: q

Exiting...
```

Notice the difference in LLM output between when the LLM was being sequentially prompted in Chat mode (>>>) in the previous chapter and when it receives a series of prompts from the Python code programmatically here. In the Chat mode, the LLM maintains knowledge of the earlier prompts and can correctly figure out the context of the question. However, when prompted programmatically, it does not remember the earlier prompts when prompted from within the Python program. So, the LLM does not inherently maintain the prompt sequence information. Let us modify the Python code to help out the LLM. The code is modified slightly to concatenate the sequence of input prompts and present them to the LLM, which allows the model to remember the context of the conversation and provide the desired answer.

```
$ cat chapter4.2.py
```

```python
# Import necessary libraries
import requests  # For sending HTTP requests to the Ollama
server

# Define the URL endpoint where the Ollama server is listening
OLLAMA_API_URL = "http://localhost:11434/api/generate"

# Print an introduction message for the user
print("Interactive Llama 3.1 Chatbot")
print("Type 'q' to exit.\n")

# Initialize the 'prompt' variable as an empty string
# This will accumulate the full conversation history (user
inputs)
prompt = ""

# Start an infinite loop to allow continuous chatting
while True:
    # Prompt the user for their input
    inp = input("You: ")

    # Check if the user wants to exit the chat
    if inp == 'q':
        print("Exiting...")  # Notify the user that the chat
is closing
        break  # Exit the while loop, thus ending the program

    # Append the new user input to the existing conversation
    # Add a newline after each input to keep the conversation
readable for the model
    prompt += inp + "\n"

    # Prepare the data (payload) that will be sent to the
Ollama server
    payload = {
        "model": "llama3.1",  # Specify the LLM model to use
        "prompt": prompt,      # Send the full accumulated
conversation so far
        "stream": False      # Set to False to receive a full
response at once (not chunked/streamed)
    }

    try:
```

```
        # Send the POST request to the Ollama server with the
payload as JSON
        response = requests.post(OLLAMA_API_URL, json=payload)

        # If the server responds with status 200 (OK)
        if response.status_code == 200:
            # Parse the JSON response
            result = response.json()

            # Display the model's generated response
            # Use .get() to avoid KeyError if "response" key
is missing
            print("Llama 3.1:", result.get("response", "No
response received."))
        else:
            # If server returned an error (not status 200),
print error details
            print("Error:", response.status_code,
response.text)

    except requests.exceptions.RequestException as e:
        # Handle possible exceptions like connection errors,
timeouts, etc.
        print("Error connecting to Ollama server:", e)
```

Now run the program:

`$ python3 chapter4.2.py`

```
Interactive Llama 3.1 Chatbot

Type 'q' to exit.


You: what is the capital of france?

Llama 3.1: The capital of France is Paris.

You: and england?

Llama 3.1: The capitals are:


1. France: **Paris**
```

```
2. England: **London** (Note: England is a part of the United
Kingdom, and London is also the capital of the UK. However, if
you're referring specifically to the country of England, I'd be
happy to provide more context!)

You: q

Exiting...
```

Context in LLMs

While prompts guide the LLM, context defines the model's cumulative "memory" during an interactive user session. Context is the accumulated information that the model uses to interpret the next user input. Every time you send a message to an LLM, the model looks at all the tokens (words, symbols, or parts of words) provided within the context window—a fixed-size buffer that determines how much text the model can "see" at once.

What Is a Context Window?

A context window is the maximum number of tokens an LLM can process in a single request. For example:

- On Ollama, LLaMA 3.1 (8B) supports up to 128,000 tokens of context.
- On their respective cloud platforms, GPT-4o and Claude 3.5 can extend to 256,000 tokens or more.

If your prompt (including prior conversation) exceeds that limit, the model will truncate older parts, effectively "forgetting" earlier messages.

How LLMs Use Context

When you interact with an LLM in chat mode, each new user input is appended to the conversation history. The model processes the entire sequence—your question, its prior answers, and the surrounding dialogue—to generate the next response. However, in stateless or programmatic prompting (like sending API requests), the model sees only the current prompt and has no built-in memory unless you explicitly include prior conversation history.

Managing Context Size

Each LLM has a fixed maximum context length, often configurable at runtime. If your conversation becomes too long, you can summarize older portions or truncate them to stay within the model's limit.

You can often set the maximum context size of your model by creating a new model based on the original model, as shown in Chapter 2.

First create the model file called **Modelfile** with this entry:

FROM llama3.1

PARAMETER num_ctx 262144

Then execute the command:

```
$ ollama create big_ctx_llama3.1 -f Modelfile

gathering model components

using existing layer
sha256:667b0c1932bc6ffc593ed1d03f895bf2dc8dc6df21db3042284a6f4416b06
a29

using existing layer
sha256:948af2743fc78a328dcb3b0f5a31b3d75f415840fdb699e8b1235978392ec
f85

using existing layer
sha256:0ba8f0e314b4264dfd19df045cde9d4c394a52474bf92ed6a3de22a4ca31a
177

creating new layer
sha256:a92aeb01f7ae8ae3ed71605f93aba7351a5f822c7f6c362f033a8c5d10860
a62

writing manifest

success


$ ollama list

NAME                    ID          SIZE    MODIFIED
```

```
big_ctx_llama3.1:latest    dab23ff2e1fb    4.9 GB    About a minute
ago

llama3.1:latest            46e0c10c039e    4.9 GB    5 hours ago

ollama show big_ctx_llama3.1:latest
  Model
    architecture        llama
    parameters          8.0B
    context length      131072
    embedding length    4096
    quantization        Q4_K_M


  Capabilities
    completion
    tools


  Parameters
    num_ctx    262144
    stop       "<|start_header_id|>"
    stop       "<|end_header_id|>"
    stop       "<|eot_id|>"


  License
    LLAMA 3.1 COMMUNITY LICENSE AGREEMENT
    Llama 3.1 Version Release Date: July 23, 2024
    ...


$ ollama run big_ctx_llama3.1:latest
>>> Send a message (/? for help)
```

You are now running big_ctx_llama3.1:latest model with a context size of 256K (262144/1024) that was created based on the original llama3.1:latest with the default context size of 128K.

The key takeaways from this chapter are:

- Prompting guides what the LLM should do.
- Context determines what the LLM remembers.
- Chat sessions retain context automatically.
- Programmatic interactions require manual context passing.
- Manage context size to prevent truncation.
- Large-context models enable long document reasoning and multi-turn dialogues.

In the next chapter, we introduce a Python library called LangChain, which has many useful features that allow easy integration of LLM interaction into Python programs. One of its features is the LangChain Memory, which helps maintain a conversation's context.

5: LangChain - Framework for Building LLM Applications

LangChain is an open-source framework designed to simplify the development of applications that need to leverage Large Language Models (LLMs). It provides an easy and consistent way to integrate LLMs, both running on local workstations and in the cloud, with external data sources, tools, and reasoning capabilities, making it ideal for building advanced AI-powered applications such as chatbots, autonomous agents, and retrieval-augmented generation (RAG) systems.

The LangChain library provides a framework to easily manage inputs to the LLM and chain different tasks together, including branching and multi-step agentic workflows. It offers powerful abstractions through Lang Chain Execution Language (LCEL) to make the process seamless. You can visit www.langchain.com to learn more about LangChain library. The Docs section from the website menu describes detailed interfaces to the library for both Python and JavaScript.

Key Features of LangChain

Listed below are some of the main functionalities provided by the LangChain library

- Prompt Management: LangChain helps structure and manage prompts, making it easier to create reusable, modular, and optimized interactions with LLMs with prompt templates that allow for multi-variable substitution of prompting text during runtime.
- Chains: The framework allows developers to create sequences of actions (chains) that involve multiple steps, such as calling an API, querying a database, or reasoning over data including parallel executions and decision branches.
- Memory: It supports short-term and long-term memory, enabling applications to maintain context across separate interactions with the LLM.
- Agents: LangChain enables dynamic decision-making by allowing LLMs to choose and execute actions using external scripts. Agents are such an

important component that we dedicate a separate chapter to this functionality.

- Retrieval & Augmentation: It facilitates access to knowledge bases, vector stores, and databases to enhance responses with external information. We also devote an entire chapter to RAG.
- Tool Integration: Supports various integrations, including APIs, search engines, calculators, and custom functions, making applications more powerful. We look at this functionality in the chapter on Agents.

Getting Started with LangChain

First install needed Python modules to run LangChain.

```
$ pip install langchain langchain_community  langchain_core
langchain_ollama
```

Prompt Templates

LangChain makes interaction with LLMs very easy by providing templates for prompts that the LLM can understand and act on. One way to create prompts is to make use of structured prompts. The LLM understands three types of structured prompts. These are, SystemMessage, AIMessage, and HumanMessage. You can stitch together these three prompt types inside one or more message structures and send them to the LLM. Structured prompts make identifying and maintaining communication boundaries between the LLM and the user easier. Prompt templates also allow one or more embedded variables in curly brackets like {replace}, which are substituted at run-time by the application for the human or AI-generated text. The LLMs are also smart enough to understand somewhat unstructured prompts; we will also use them in later examples.

```
$ cat chapter5-1.py
```

```
# Import necessary message classes from LangChain Core
from langchain_core.messages import AIMessage, HumanMessage,
SystemMessage

# Import the Ollama LLM (Large Language Model) interface from
LangChain's Ollama module
```

```python
from langchain_ollama import OllamaLLM

# Initialize the LLaMA Model
# Create an instance of the OllamaLLM object
# - Specify which model to use ("llama3.1")
# - Provide the base URL where the Ollama server is running
locally
llama = OllamaLLM(model="llama3.1",
base_url="http://localhost:11434")

# Set Up Initial Conversation Messages
# Prepare a list of messages to send to the model
# Message sequence is very important in LangChain conversation
chains

messages = [
    SystemMessage(content="Print answer in CAPS"),  #
Instruction to the model (sets behavior for responses)
    HumanMessage(content="What is the capital of UK?"),  #
User's input/question to the model
]

# Print the list of prepared messages (for
debugging/visualization)
print(messages)

# First Model Invocation
# Invoke (send) the messages to the LLaMA model
# The model will process the message history and return a
response
result = llama.invoke(messages)

# Optionally check type of 'messages' list (commented out)
# print(type(messages))

# Print the model's response to the initial prompt
print(result)

# Extend the conversation by:
# - Adding the model's previous response as an AIMessage (this
simulates the AI replying)
# - Adding a new HumanMessage asking to expand on the answer
messages = messages + [AIMessage(content=result)] +
[HumanMessage(content="Also add the capital of France to the
answer")]

# Print the updated list of messages to see the expanded
conversation history
print(messages)
```

```
# Second Model Invocation
# Send the updated (longer) conversation history back to the
model
# This allows the model to incorporate prior responses + new
user instructions into its output
result = llama.invoke(messages)

# Print the model's final response based on the expanded
conversation
print(result)
```

Now run the program:

```
$ python3 chapter5-1.py
```

[SystemMessage(content='Print answer in CAPS', additional_kwargs={}, response_metadata={}), **HumanMessage(content='What is the capital of UK?'**, additional_kwargs={}, response_metadata={})]

LONDON

[SystemMessage(content='Print answer in CAPS', additional_kwargs={}, response_metadata={}), HumanMessage(content='What is the capital of UK?', additional_kwargs={}, response_metadata={}), **AIMessage(content='LONDON'**, additional_kwargs={}, response_metadata={}), HumanMessage(content='Also add the capital of France to the answer', additional_kwargs={}, response_metadata={})]

LONDON PARIS

Notice that after the initial LLM invocation, we extended the message structure by adding the AI response AIMessage(content='LONDON' to the list which preserves the context of the chat.

Chains and LangChain Execution Language (LCEL)

LangChain Execution Language (LCEL) is a declarative way to compose and execute chains of tasks, logic, and interactions with LLMs. It allows you to structure model calls, transformations, and memory persistence in a simple yet powerful syntax, hiding complexities through simple abstractions that is described as a sequence of steps connected by the pipe (|) symbol. Here's an example using LCEL to compose a sequence of operations.

```python
# Import required classes from LangChain and LangChain-Ollama
from langchain_ollama import OllamaLLM  # Interface to
communicate with a local Ollama LLM server
from langchain_core.prompts import ChatPromptTemplate,
PromptTemplate  # To create prompt templates
from langchain_core.output_parsers import StrOutputParser  #
To parse model outputs into strings
from langchain_core.runnables import RunnablePassthrough  # A
passthrough node used in LCEL chains

# Model Initialization
# Create an instance of the LLaMA model
# - Specify the model name ("llama3.1")
# - Provide the base URL where the Ollama server is running
llama = OllamaLLM(model="llama3.1",
base_url="http://localhost:11434")


# Without Using LCEL (Direct Prompting)
######################################
# Define an **unstructured prompt template** for a simple
question
# This will later be formatted with a specific country name
template = "What is the capital of {country}?"
prompt_template = ChatPromptTemplate.from_template(template)
# Create a ChatPromptTemplate from the raw template string

# Format the prompt by substituting the {country} variable
# Note: We use .format() to fill in "France" dynamically
prompt = prompt_template.format(country="France")

# Send the formatted prompt directly to the LLM and get a
response
result = llama.invoke(prompt)

# Print the model's output
print("No LCEL: ", result)


# Using LCEL (LangChain Expression Language)
############################################

# Define a structured PromptTemplate using LCEL conventions
```

60

```
# This template again defines a question about a country's
capital
prompt = PromptTemplate.from_template("What is capital of
{country}?")

# Define an LCEL **Chain** using operators (|) to link
multiple components
# Here's how the chain works:
# - RunnablePassthrough(): Initially passes the input without
modifying it
# - prompt: Formats the input into a structured prompt
# - llama: Sends the formatted prompt to the LLM for a
response
# - StrOutputParser(): Extracts and formats the final output
as a clean string
chain = (
    RunnablePassthrough()
    | prompt
    | llama
    | StrOutputParser()
)

# Execute the chain by providing an input dictionary
# LCEL automatically maps the "country" key to the {country}
placeholder
response = chain.invoke({"country": "France"})

# Print the output generated by the model using the LCEL chain
print("Using LCEL: ", response)
```

Now run the program:

```
$ python3 chapter5-2.py
```

No LCEL: The capital of France is Paris.

Using LCEL: The capital of France is Paris.

The program above has two sections. In the first section, we do not make use of LCEL and chain, but in the next section, we make use of the chain abstraction by simply piping a sequence of steps using the pipe (|) symbol.

```
chain = (
    RunnablePassthrough()
    | prompt  # Format input with prompt template
    | llama   # Send formatted input to the model
    | StrOutputParser()  # Parse output as a string
)
```

In our code, we set up the chain in the following way. First, we call RunnablePassthrough(), and then the prompt is generated, after which the model is invoked with the generated prompt. Finally, the StrOutputParser() function removes all the metadata returned from the model invocation. The remaining output from the model is then printed out. Once set up, the chain is executed by the invoke call. Above is a tiny program; therefore, chain abstraction only adds marginal clarity to the code; however, when we have a program that needs complex chaining, parallel execution, and other functionality, including decision paths, the use of LCEL will be indispensable.

To create the chain, we used the RunnablePassthrough interface from the Runnable class, which is the core class for setting up pipelines and multi-step workflows in LangChain. Among other available interfaces is RunnableLambda, which we can use to create custom runnable functions in Python. Other functions allow tasks to be run in parallel and create branching logic in the code.

Runnable Type	Purpose
RunnablePassthrough	Directly passes input as output
RunnableLambda	Allows using custom Python functions
RunnableMap	Runs multiple functions on different parts of input in parallel
RunnableSequence	Chains multiple steps sequentially
RunnableBranch	Implements conditional branching logic
RunnableParallel	Runs multiple functions in parallel with the same input
RunnableEach	Applies a function to each element in a list
RunnableRetry	Retries failed executions with a specified policy

Table 5.1: List of the Runnable types

Extending the chain with RunnableLambda

It is easy to add to the functionality of a chain by incorporation your own Python function using the RunnableLambda interface.

```
$ cat chapter5-3.py
```

```
# Import necessary classes and functions from LangChain and
LangChain-Ollama

from langchain_ollama import OllamaLLM  # Interface to
communicate with the Ollama LLM server
from langchain_core.prompts import ChatPromptTemplate,
PromptTemplate  # Tools for creating text prompt templates
from langchain_core.output_parsers import StrOutputParser  #
Parses model responses into plain strings
from langchain_core.runnables import RunnablePassthrough,
RunnableLambda  # Tools for building LCEL chains

# Initialize the LLaMA Model
# Create an instance of the LLaMA model from Ollama
# - Specify the model name ("llama3.1")
# - Set the base URL of the locally running Ollama server
llama = OllamaLLM(model="llama3.1",
base_url="http://localhost:11434")


# Define the Prompt Template
# Create a structured PromptTemplate
# The template defines a simple question, where {country} will
be dynamically replaced
prompt = PromptTemplate.from_template("What is capital of
{country}?")


# Define a Lambda Function to Post-process Output
# Define a RunnableLambda that modifies the output from the
LLM
# - The lambda function takes a string 'x' and converts it to
all UPPERCASE letters
# - This step post-processes the LLM output before final
presentation
capitalize_output = RunnableLambda(lambda x: x.upper())
```

```
# Build the LCEL Chain
# LCEL (LangChain Expression Language) Chain:
# This defines a sequence of operations, linked together using
the '|' operator

chain = (
    RunnablePassthrough()   # 1. Initially passes input
unchanged (raw dictionary {"country": "France"})
    | prompt                # 2. Formats the input into a full
prompt string using the template
    | llama                 # 3. Sends the formatted prompt to
the LLaMA model and retrieves a response
    | StrOutputParser()     # 4. Parses the raw model output
into a simple string
    | capitalize_output     # 5. Applies the lambda function to
capitalize the final response
)


# Execute the Chain
# Provide the input value ("France") mapped to the variable
{country}
response = chain.invoke({"country": "France"})

# Print the final processed output (which will be capitalized)
print(response)
```

Run the program:

```
$ python3 chapter5-3.py
```

THE CAPITAL OF FRANCE IS PARIS.

For this program, we defined a Python Lambda function **capitalize_output** using the **RunnableLambda** interface that takes the output from the previous chain step, call to **StrOutputParser()**, which filters out the resulting string from the model invocation and capitalizes it. This way, we can perform any number of tasks at the start, middle, or end of the chain by writing our own Python functions.

Parallel chains with RunnableParallel

Although a chain implies sequential execution of tasks, sometimes the workflow must execute several tasks in parallel, which is possible with the RunnableParallel interface. In the following program, AI acts as a nutrition expert and helps us gather a health supplement's good and bad characteristics (Vitamin B12). Here, the program first gathers the list of all traits (the first LLM call), then launches two parallel chains to collect the good and bad characteristics separately, and in the last step, combines the two separately generated lists and prints out the combined list.

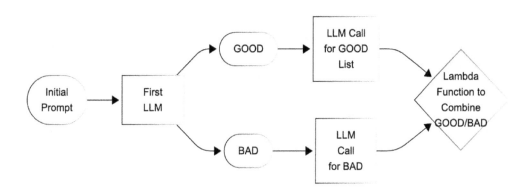

Figure 5.1: RunnableParallel

```
$ cat chapter5-4.py
```

```
# Import necessary modules from LangChain and LangChain-Ollama
from langchain_ollama import OllamaLLM  # Interface for
calling a local Ollama LLM server
from langchain_core.prompts import ChatPromptTemplate  # For
defining structured chat-style prompts
from langchain_core.output_parsers import StrOutputParser  #
To parse model outputs as plain strings
from langchain_core.runnables import RunnableLambda,
RunnableParallel, RunnablePassthrough  # Tools for building
LCEL chains

# Initialize the LLaMA Model
# Create an instance of the LLaMA model (Llama 3.1)
```

```python
# - 'base_url' points to the local Ollama server
llama = OllamaLLM(model="llama3.1",
base_url="http://localhost:11434")


# Define Initial Prompt Template
# Define a chat prompt that sets the system role as a
nutrition expert
# Human input requests listing good and bad features of a
given product
prompt_template = ChatPromptTemplate.from_messages([
    ("system", "You are a nutrition expert."),  # System
message to set model's role
    ("human", "List the main characteristics, both good and
bad, of this {product}.")  # User instruction with a
placeholder
])


# Define the Initial Feature Extraction Chain
# Create the first chain:
# 1. Format the input product name using the prompt template
# 2. Send the formatted prompt to the LLaMA model
# 3. Parse the output as a plain string
initial_chain = (
    prompt_template
    | llama
    | StrOutputParser()
)

# Run the initial chain by providing a specific product
("Vitamin B12")
# The result will contain all (good + bad) characteristics
first_result = initial_chain.invoke({"product": "Vitamin
B12"})


# Define Good Characteristics Extraction Chain
# Define a helper function to generate a prompt focusing only
on good features
def get_good_prompts(features):
    good_template = ChatPromptTemplate.from_messages([
        ("system", "You are a nutrition expert."),
        ("human", f"Given these features, {features}, list
only the good characteristics. Limit the list to 3 items."),
    ])
    return good_template.format_prompt(features=features)

# Define a chain that:
# 1. Takes the initial features
# 2. Formats a "good characteristics" prompt
```

```python
# 3. Sends it to the LLM
# 4. Parses the output
good_chain = (
    RunnableLambda(lambda x: get_good_prompts(x))
    | llama
    | StrOutputParser()
)


# Execute the good features extraction separately (optional
step)
good_result = good_chain.invoke(first_result)


# Define Bad Characteristics Extraction Chain
# Define a helper function to generate a prompt focusing only
on bad features
def get_bad_prompts(features):
    bad_template = ChatPromptTemplate.from_messages([
        ("system", "You are a nutrition expert."),
        ("human", f"Given these features, {features}, list
only the bad characteristics. Limit the list to 3."),
    ])
    return bad_template.format_prompt(features=features)


# Define a chain that:
# 1. Takes the initial features
# 2. Formats a "bad characteristics" prompt
# 3. Sends it to the LLM
# 4. Parses the output
bad_chain = (
    RunnableLambda(lambda x: get_bad_prompts(x))
    | llama
    | StrOutputParser()
)


# Execute the bad features extraction separately (optional
step)
bad_result = bad_chain.invoke(first_result)


# Define Combination Function
# Helper function to combine good and bad characteristics into
a formatted string
def combine_good_bad(good, bad):
    return f"Good: \n{good}\n\nBad:\n{bad}"


# Define the Full Parallel Chain
# Full chain overview:
# 1. Format the initial product prompt
```

```
# 2. Send to the LLaMA model to get all features
# 3. Parse initial output
# 4. Split the output into two branches ("good" and "bad")
processed in parallel
# 5. Combine the results into a single string

full_chain = (
    prompt_template  # Format the initial product prompt
    | llama           # Query the model
    | StrOutputParser()   # Parse model response
    | RunnableParallel(branches={"good": good_chain, "bad":
bad_chain})  # Run good and bad extractions in parallel
    | RunnableLambda(lambda x:
combine_good_bad(x["branches"]["good"], x["branches"]["bad"]))
# Combine the results
)


# Execute the Full Chain
# Provide the initial input ("Vitamin B12")
# - The full chain extracts, separates, and combines good and
bad features
result = full_chain.invoke({"product": "Vitamin B12"})

# Print the final combined output
print("*****************====>FULL CHAIN: ", result)
```

Run the program:

```
$ python3 chapter5-4.py
```

*****************====>FULL CHAIN: Good:

Here are the top 3 Good Characteristics of Vitamin B12:

1. **Energy Production**: Vitamin B12 is necessary for the
production of red blood cells, which carry oxygen throughout the
body and give energy to our muscles.

2. **Nervous System Function**: It's essential for the synthesis of
myelin, the fatty substance that surrounds nerve fibers,
facilitating proper nerve function and communication.

3. **Mood Support**: Vitamin B12 deficiency has been linked to
depression, anxiety, and other mood disorders, making
supplementation essential for maintaining mental health.

```
:Bad:

Here are the 3 "Bad Characteristics" of Vitamin B12:


1. **Deficiency Commonality**: Vitamin B12 deficiency is relatively
common, affecting approximately 10% to 20% of older adults in
developed countries.

2. **High Tissue Storage**: Unlike other vitamins, vitamin B12 can
accumulate in tissues over time, potentially leading to toxicity
with excessive intake or prolonged high levels.

3. **Anemia Risk**: Prolonged vitamin B12 deficiency can lead to
anemia, characterized by fatigue, weakness, and shortness of breath.
```

Note the two branches embedded in the RunnableParallel call:

```
RunnableParallel(branches={"good": good_chain, "bad":
bad_chain})
```

Branching Execution with RunnableBranch

In LangChain, RunnableBranch interface enables conditional execution of different processing paths based on input conditions. It acts like an **if-elif-else** decision tree, where different execution chains are triggered based on specific conditions. This is how RunnableBranch works:

- You define multiple condition-function pairs, where each function determines whether the corresponding chain should run.
- The first condition that evaluates to True will determine the execution branch.
- If no conditions match, an optional default chain runs.

The Python program below demonstrates this mechanism. The AI is asked to act as a helpful grocery store assistant. When the customer asks it where to find meat, vegetable, or dairy products in the store, based on the type of the produce the customer is looking to buy, the AI answers in a helpful way to guide the customer. In case the product this customer wants to buy is not meat, vegetable or dairy, the AI directs her to the customer service department.

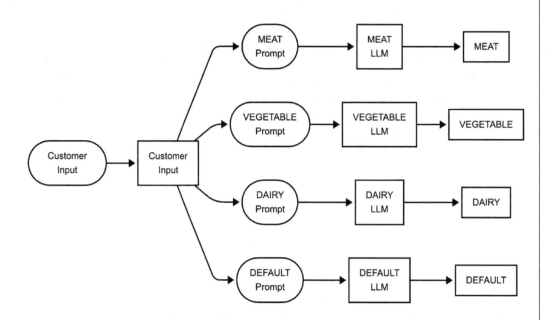

Figure 5.2: RunnableBranch

```
$ cat chapter5-5.py
```

```
# Import necessary modules
from langchain_core.prompts import ChatPromptTemplate  # For
creating structured prompt templates
from langchain_core.output_parsers import StrOutputParser  #
To parse model output into plain strings
from langchain_ollama import OllamaLLM  # Interface to
interact with a local Ollama LLM server
from langchain_core.runnables import RunnableBranch  # For
conditional branching based on model output

# Initialize the Model
# Create an instance of the LLaMA model
```

```python
# - 'model' specifies the model version (Llama 3.1)
# - 'base_url' points to your locally running Ollama server
llama = OllamaLLM(model="llama3.1",
base_url="http://localhost:11434")


# Define Prompt Templates for Different Product Types
# Template for products related to MEAT
meat_product_template = ChatPromptTemplate.from_messages([
    ("system", "You are a grocery store assistant."),
    ("human", "Direct the shopper to the meat department if
she is looking for meat products: {product}.")
])

# Template for products related to VEGETABLES
vegetable_product_template =
ChatPromptTemplate.from_messages([
    ("system", "You are a grocery store assistant."),
    ("human", "Direct the shopper to the vegetable department
if she is looking for vegetables: {product}.")
])

# Template for products related to DAIRY
dairy_product_template = ChatPromptTemplate.from_messages([
    ("system", "You are a grocery store assistant."),
    ("human", "Direct the shopper to the dairy department if
she is looking for dairy: {product}.")
])

# Default template for OTHER products (not meat, vegetable, or
dairy)
customer_service_template = ChatPromptTemplate.from_messages([
    ("system", "You are a grocery store assistant."),
    ("human", "Direct the shopper to the customer service
department if she is not looking for meat, vegetable or dairy:
{product}.")
])

# Define Classification Prompt Template
# Template that asks the model to classify the customer's
requested product
product_classification_template =
ChatPromptTemplate.from_messages([
    ("system", "You are a grocery store assistant."),
    ("human", "Classify the customer product as meat,
vegetable, dairy, or customer service: {product}.")
])

# Define Branches Based on Product Classification
# RunnableBranch handles conditional logic:
```

```python
# Based on the classification, it routes the flow to the
correct prompt and response chain
branches = RunnableBranch(
    (
        lambda x: "meat" in x,  # If 'meat' is in the model's
classification
        meat_product_template | llama | StrOutputParser()
    ),
    (
        lambda x: "vegetable" in x,  # If 'vegetable' is in
the model's classification
        vegetable_product_template | llama | StrOutputParser()
    ),
    (
        lambda x: "dairy" in x,  # If 'dairy' is in the
model's classification
        dairy_product_template | llama | StrOutputParser()
    ),
    # Default branch (fallback if none of the above match)
    customer_service_template | llama | StrOutputParser()
)

# Define the Classification Chain
# First classify the product using the classification template
product_classification_chain = product_classification_template
| llama | StrOutputParser()

# Chain together classification and branching
# 1. Classify the input
# 2. Based on the classification, follow the correct branch
chain = product_classification_chain | branches

# Simulate Conversations and Test Different Scenarios
# ----- Test 1: Meat Product -----
customer_request_meat = "Hi, I am looking for honey ham, where
will I find it?"
result = chain.invoke({"product": customer_request_meat})
print("Meat Request: ", result)

# ----- Test 2: Vegetable Product -----
customer_request_vegetable = "Do you sell french cut beans?"
result = chain.invoke({"product": customer_request_vegetable})
print("Vegetable Request: ", result)

# ----- Test 3: Dairy Product -----
customer_request_dairy = "Hello, I need some greek yogurt, do
you have any?"
result = chain.invoke({"product": customer_request_dairy})
print("Dairy Request: ", result)
```

```
# ----- Test 4: Default (Other Product) -----
customer_request_default = "Do you sell band-aid?"
result = chain.invoke({"product": customer_request_default})
print("Not Meat, Vegetable or Dairy Request: ", result)
```

Now run the program:

```
$ python3 chapter5-5.py
```

Are you looking for any specific items today?

If you're looking for meat products, we have a wide selection in the
meat department. You can find it to your left as you enter the
store. We also have a deli section located at the back of the store
if you're interested in freshly prepared meats or sandwiches.

Is there anything else I can help you with?

Vegetable Request: Welcome to our grocery store! I'd be happy to
help you find what you're looking for. What can I assist you with
today?

If you're not looking for meat, vegetables, or dairy products, it
might be best to head over to the customer service department.
They'll be able to answer any general questions you may have about
our store or direct you to where you need to go.

However, if you are looking for something specific in those
categories, I'd be happy to help you navigate the aisles and find
what you're looking for. What's on your shopping list today?

Dairy Request: "Hi there! Welcome to our store. We have a wide
selection of products, but I can help you find what you're looking
for. You mentioned you're looking for something in the dairy
section? Let me show you where that is. It's just down this aisle,
first shelf on your right."

Not Meat, Vegetable or Dairy Request: The Band-Aid would be best
directed to the Customer Service department. Would you like me to
escort you there?

```
```

The structure of the "branching" code above with RunnableBranch() interface is intuitive and elegant. Specific branches in the code look for the three products: meat, dairy, and vegetables, and the default branch if the product the customer seeks is not one of the three mentioned, which directs her to customer service for more help.

LangChain Memory using ConversationBufferMemory

The LangChain memory feature solves state persistence problems when interacting with Language Models programmatically. Here are the key issues it addresses:

- Lack of Context Retention in Stateless LLMs: Traditional LLM calls are stateless, meaning they do not remember past interactions. LangChain memory enables conversational AI to retain past exchanges, allowing for coherent, context-aware conversations.
- Enhancing User Experience with Personalized Interactions: Users often want personalized and dynamic interactions over multiple interactions. Memory can store and recall user preferences, past choices, and other relevant details.
- Enabling Agents & Task Execution Over Multiple Steps: Some workflows (e.g., reasoning, planning, agent execution) require past outputs to guide future steps. Memory enables stateful agents that track progress across multiple steps.

```
$ cat chapter5-6.py
```

```
# Import Required Modules
from langchain_community.chat_message_histories import
ChatMessageHistory  # To store and retrieve conversation
history
from langchain_core.prompts import PromptTemplate  # To create
structured prompt templates
```

```python
from langchain_core.runnables import RunnablePassthrough,
RunnableLambda  # For building LCEL (LangChain Expression
Language) chains
from langchain_core.output_parsers import StrOutputParser  #
To parse model responses into clean strings
from langchain_ollama import OllamaLLM  # Interface to
interact with the locally running Ollama server
from langchain_core.messages import HumanMessage, AIMessage  #
Message types


# Initialize the LLM Model
# Create an instance of the LLaMA model (Llama 3.1) hosted
locally via Ollama
llama = OllamaLLM(model="llama3.1",
base_url="http://localhost:11434")


# Set Up Conversation Memory
# Initialize a ChatMessageHistory object to keep track of the
conversation messages
chat_history = ChatMessageHistory()


# Define Helper Function to Format Chat History
# Define a function that formats the stored chat history for
input into the prompt
def format_chat_history(input_data):
    """
    Formats the conversation history into a readable text
block
    and returns it along with the new user input.

    Args:
        input_data (dict): Contains the new user input.

    Returns:
        dict: A dictionary with 'chat_history' and 'input'
keys.
    """
    # Retrieve all previous messages from chat history
    history = chat_history.messages

    # Format each message like "Human: message_content" or
"Ai: message_content"
    formatted_history = "\n".join(
        [f"{msg.type.capitalize()}: {msg.content}" for msg in
history]
    )
```

```python
        # Return a dictionary expected by the prompt template
    return {"chat_history": formatted_history, "input":
input_data["input"]}


# Define the Prompt Template
# Create a prompt template that structures the chat history
and the current user input
# '{chat_history}' will be replaced by the formatted past
conversation
# '{input}' will be replaced by the current user input
prompt = PromptTemplate.from_template("{chat_history}\nHuman:
{input}\nAssistant:")


# Build the LCEL Chain
# Build the chain by linking components together:
chain = (
    RunnablePassthrough()  # Pass input directly into the
chain without modification
    | RunnableLambda(format_chat_history)  # Apply the
format_chat_history function to structure history + input
    | prompt  # Format it using the PromptTemplate
    | llama  # Send the formatted prompt to the LLaMA model
    | StrOutputParser()  # Parse the raw model response into a
plain string
)


# Simulate a Conversation
# Step 1: Ask a question about France
user_input_1 = "What is the capital of France?"
response_1 = chain.invoke({"input": user_input_1})
print(response_1)

# Save the conversation to chat history
chat_history.add_message(HumanMessage(content=user_input_1))
chat_history.add_message(AIMessage(content=response_1))


# Step 2: Ask a question about India
user_input_2 = "Btw, can you also provide the name of the
capital of India?"
response_2 = chain.invoke({"input": user_input_2})
print(response_2)

# Save the conversation to chat history
chat_history.add_message(HumanMessage(content=user_input_2))
chat_history.add_message(AIMessage(content=response_2))
```

```
# Step 3: Request to show the last two answers line by line
user_input_3 = "Show the last two answers in a new line."
response_3 = chain.invoke({"input": user_input_3})
print(response_3)

# Save the conversation to chat history
chat_history.add_message(HumanMessage(content=user_input_3))
chat_history.add_message(AIMessage(content=response_3))


# Step 4: Request to repeat the answers but in all capital
letters
user_input_4 = "Please provide the answers again in CAPS."
response_4 = chain.invoke({"input": user_input_4})
print(response_4)

# Save the conversation to chat history
chat_history.add_message(HumanMessage(content=user_input_4))
chat_history.add_message(AIMessage(content=response_4))
```

Now run the program:

```
$ python3 chapter5-6.py
```

```
Paris.

New Delhi.

Paris

New Delhi

PARIS

NEW DELHI
```

In this program, the **ChatMessageHistory** class and its associated method **add_message** are used to incrementally maintain the context of a chat with the LLM up to that point in time. Without this ability to recall and reuse the conversation with the LLM, we cannot request the LLM to "CAN YOU ALSO PROVIDE THE NAME OF THE CAPITAL OF INDIA?" Since the LLM is stateless, without the help of the memory functions, the LLM will not remember that we asked about the capital of France earlier; therefore, we will not be able to add the capital of India to2 the list of capitals.

6: LLM Application Usecases

One of the best ways to explore how LangChain works is through few more use cases. Below are four Python programs illustrating how you can use LangChain to interact with the LLaMA 3.1 model running on the Ollama server on a local workstation. The programs below highlight how LangChain can be used in various contexts where LLMs need to be integrated into larger applications or workflows.

Text Summarization - Summarizing long documents or articles into shorter, more digestible content.

You can use LangChain to create a summary of a long document or text.

```
$ cat chapter6-1.py
```

```
# Import Required Modules
from langchain_core.prompts import PromptTemplate  # For
creating text prompt templates
from langchain_ollama import OllamaLLM  # Interface to
communicate with the local Ollama LLM server


# Initialize the LLaMA Model
# Create an instance of the LLaMA model
# - 'model' specifies the model name ("llama3.1")
# - 'base_url' points to the local server where the Ollama
service is running
llama = OllamaLLM(model="llama3.1",
base_url="http://localhost:11434")


# Define the Prompt Template
# Create a PromptTemplate for summarization tasks
# - 'input_variables' defines which variables are expected to
fill the template
# - 'template' defines the actual prompt text with a
placeholder for dynamic input
prompt = PromptTemplate(
    input_variables=["text"],  # Placeholder variable name
    template="Summarize the following text in fifty words:
{text}"  # Prompt directing LLM to 50 word summary
```

```
)

# Build the Summarization Chain
# Create a chain by connecting the prompt directly to the
model
# Using LangChain's operator (|) syntax:
# - Pass the formatted prompt output directly as input into
the LLaMA model
summarize_chain = prompt | llama


# Define the Input Text (~250 words)
# # Text that you want the model to summarize
text = (
    "The advent of Large Language Models (LLMs) has
transformed how organizations think about artificial
intelligence. "
    "Rather than building narrow AI solutions for specific
tasks, companies can now use LLMs as general-purpose engines
capable of adapting to a wide range of needs, "
    "from customer support automation to creative writing
assistance. "
    "However, deploying these models effectively requires more
than just access to powerful algorithms; it demands thoughtful
integration into real-world workflows.\n\n"

    "LangChain is a leading open-source Python framework that
helps developers bridge this gap. "
    "By offering modular building blocks such as prompt
templates, memory management systems, agent creation,
retrieval-augmented generation (RAG) pipelines, "
    "and multi-modal tool integration, LangChain enables
developers to create dynamic applications that leverage the
full power of LLMs while remaining customizable to specific
business goals.\n\n"

    "Beyond technical tooling, LangChain also promotes
responsible AI usage. It encourages incorporating retrieval
systems to ground answers in trusted documents, "
    "thus reducing hallucination risks, and supports
conversation memory to maintain context across multi-turn
dialogues.\n\n"

    "As enterprises and startups alike explore the potential
of LLM-driven applications, frameworks like LangChain are
becoming essential. "
    "They not only speed up prototyping but also pave the way
for production-grade deployments by offering standardized
patterns and best practices. "
```

```
    "In a rapidly evolving AI landscape, mastering tools like
LangChain will likely be a key differentiator for developers
and organizations seeking to stay ahead."
)


# Execute the Chain
# Invoke the summarization chain by providing the input text
# - 'invoke' takes a dictionary mapping input variable names
to their actual values
summary = summarize_chain.invoke({"text": text})


# Output the Result (summarized to fifty words)
# Print the summarized text produced by the model
print("Summary:", summary)
```

Now run the program:

```
$ python3 chapter6-1.py
```

```
Summary: LangChain is an open-source Python framework that helps
developers effectively integrate Large Language Models (LLMs) into
real-world workflows. It provides modular building blocks for
creating dynamic applications and promotes responsible AI usage,
enabling faster prototyping and production-grade deployments in a
rapidly evolving AI landscape.
```

Text Generation - Generating creative text, such as stories, product descriptions, or even code.

LangChain can also generate text based on a provided prompt. We asked the AI to make a short story about "a bear who does not like honey!" You can read the entire output to judge the quality of the generated tale.

```
$ cat chapter6-2.py
```

```
# Import Required Modules
```

```python
from langchain_core.prompts import PromptTemplate  # To create
structured prompt templates for the LLM
from langchain_ollama import OllamaLLM  # Interface to connect
to the locally running Ollama LLM server


# Initialize the LLaMA Model
# Create an instance of the LLaMA 3.1 model hosted locally
# - 'model' specifies the version to use
# - 'base_url' points to the local Ollama API server (running
at localhost:11434)
llama = OllamaLLM(model="llama3.1",
base_url="http://localhost:11434")


# Define the Prompt Template for Story Generation
# Define a PromptTemplate that dynamically injects a 'topic'
into a story request
# - 'input_variables' defines which variables will be passed
into the template
# - 'template' defines the text structure where the variable
{topic} will be inserted
prompt = PromptTemplate(
    input_variables=["topic"],  # The placeholder variable
name expected when running the template
    template="Write a short story about {topic}."  # How the
input will be framed when sent to the model
)


# Build the Generation Chain
# Create a LangChain Expression Language (LCEL) sequence
# - Pipe (|) connects the output of the prompt directly to the
LLaMA model
# - The prompt is formatted first, then passed into the model
for text generation
generation_chain = prompt | llama


# Execute the Chain to Generate Text
# Provide an input for the 'topic' variable and run the chain
# - 'invoke' triggers the pipeline to format the prompt and
generate a response
#generated_text = generation_chain.invoke({"topic": "a cat who
explores outer space"})
generated_text = generation_chain.invoke({"topic": "a bear who
does not like honey!"})


# Output the Generated Text
```

```
# Print the generated short story to the console
print(generated_text)
```

Now run the program:

```
$ python3 chapter6-2.py
```

In a dense forest, where the tall trees creaked and groaned with
every gentle breeze, there lived a big, fluffy bear named Bert. Bert
was a bit of an oddity among his fellow bears, for he had one
peculiar trait that set him apart from the rest: he detested honey.

While his friends would spend hours buzzing around beehives,
collecting pots and jars full of golden nectar to satisfy their
sweet tooth, Bert would turn up his nose in disgust. He preferred
the taste of ripe berries, juicy fish, or even a well-cooked
mushroom over that sticky, syrupy stuff.

As a cub, Bert's mother had tried everything to get him to enjoy
honey. She'd dangle pots under beehives, coaxing him with sweet
words and promises of a taste adventure. But no matter how hard she
tried, Bert just couldn't stand the gooey texture or the
overpowering sweetness.

The other bears found this aversion hilarious. They'd tease him
mercilessly, calling him "Honey-Hater" and "Bert the Bear-who-
doesn't-know-his-taste-buds." Even the beavers, who were notorious
honey-lovers themselves, would chuckle good-naturedly at Bert's
plight.

But Bert didn't let their jokes bother him. He knew what he liked,
and that was a diverse palate, free from the confines of one
particular flavor. He'd spend his days exploring the forest,
sniffing out hidden streams for salmon or plucking the ripest
berries from the bushes.

One summer afternoon, as Bert wandered through a sun-dappled
clearing, he stumbled upon an elderly bear named Boris. Boris was
known throughout the land for his epic honey-pairings - combinations
of sweet and savory that would make even the most discerning bears
weak in the knees. Bert had always been fascinated by Boris's
expertise but had never mustered the courage to ask for a taste.

"Ah, young Bert," said Boris, noticing the curious bear watching
from afar. "I see you're not among the honey enthusiasts like your
friends. But tell me, have you ever tried it with something else?"

Bert shook his head, intrigued by the old bear's words.

"Well," continued Boris, "honey on its own is a bit too much for most bears, but when paired with... say... a ripe pear or some roasted nuts... now that's a different story altogether."

Intrigued, Bert asked if he could try it. Boris led him to his hidden honey cache and carefully drizzled a small amount onto a ripe pear slice.

The first bite was like nothing Bert had ever experienced. The sweetness wasn't overpowering; instead, it complemented the subtle flavors of the pear perfectly. For the first time in his life, Bert began to appreciate honey's unique charm.

From that day forward, Bert and Boris became unlikely friends, experimenting with new combinations of sweet and savory until they'd created a whole new world of flavor possibilities for themselves.

The other bears watched in awe as Bert shed his "Honey-Hater" moniker and became known as the most adventurous palate in the forest. And whenever someone asked him why he loved honey so much now, he'd simply smile and say: "It's all about balance, my friends. A little bit of sweetness can go a long way — if you know where to find it."

Question Answering (QA) - Extracting answers from a large corpus or dataset based on a given question.

LangChain can be used to answer questions from a provided dataset or context. Chapter 9 provides a more powerful technique for performing similar tasks called Retrieval Augmented Generation (RAG).

```
$ cat chapter6-3.py
```

```
# Import Required Modules
from langchain_core.prompts import PromptTemplate  # For
creating structured prompts with variables
from langchain_ollama import OllamaLLM  # To interact with the
local Ollama server and run the LLaMA model


# Initialize the Ollama LLaMA Model
# Create an instance of the LLaMA model (Llama 3.1 version)
running locally
```

```
# - 'model' specifies the model name
# - 'base_url' specifies the address of the local Ollama
server
llama = OllamaLLM(model="llama3.1",
base_url="http://localhost:11434")


# Define the Question-Answering Prompt Template
# Create a PromptTemplate that accepts two variables:
'context' and 'question'
# - 'context' provides background information to help the
model answer accurately
# - 'question' is the query that the model will attempt to
answer
qa_prompt = PromptTemplate(
    input_variables=["context", "question"],  # Declare the
placeholders needed
    template="Given the following context: {context} \nAnswer
the question: {question}"  # Template structure
)


# Build the Question-Answering Chain
# Link the prompt directly to the model using LangChain's
piping syntax (| operator)
# - The chain will format the inputs into a full prompt and
then send it to the model
qa_chain = qa_prompt | llama


# Define Context and Question
# Context: The background information that will assist the
model in answering
context = (
    "LangChain is an open-source Python framework designed to
simplify the development of applications powered by large
language models (LLMs). "
    "It provides a suite of tools for constructing complex
workflows by combining LLMs with external data sources, APIs,
memory management, and user inputs. "
    "LangChain enables developers to build sophisticated
chains, agents, retrieval-augmented generation (RAG)
pipelines, and conversational agents. "
    "By modularizing components like prompt templates,
document loaders, and vector stores, it makes LLM-powered apps
easier to build, debug, and deploy. "
    "It also promotes responsible AI practices by encouraging
grounded responses based on trusted documents, reducing
hallucination risks. "
```

```
     "LangChain has quickly become a go-to toolkit for
startups, enterprises, and researchers exploring real-world
LLM applications across industries like education, healthcare,
and finance."
)


# Question: What we want to ask the model, based on the
provided context
question = "What is LangChain?"


# Invoke the Chain to Generate the Answer
# Run the chain by passing a dictionary that maps variables to
their actual values
# - 'invoke' triggers the flow: formatting → model call →
response
answer = qa_chain.invoke({"context": context, "question":
question})


# Output the Result
# Print the model's answer to the console
print("Answer:", answer)
```

Now run the program:

```
$ python3 chapter6-3.py
```

```
Answer: LangChain is an open-source Python framework designed to
simplify the development of applications powered by large language
models (LLMs). It provides a suite of tools for constructing complex
workflows by combining LLMs with external data sources, APIs, memory
management, and user inputs.
```

Data Extraction and Transformation - Extracting structured information from unstructured text and transforming it into a usable format (e.g., JSON, CSV).

LangChain can extract data from unstructured text and transform it into
structured data.

```python
# Import Required Modules
from langchain_core.prompts import PromptTemplate  # For
creating structured prompt templates
from langchain_core.runnables import RunnableLambda  # For
creating simple runnable transformations (not used directly
here)
from langchain_ollama import ChatOllama  # To interact with a
local Ollama server for LLaMA chat-based models
from langchain_core.runnables import RunnableSequence  # For
chaining components together into a runnable sequence


# Initialize the Ollama LLaMA Model
# Create an instance of the LLaMA 3.1 chat model through
Ollama
# - 'model' specifies the model name
# - 'base_url' points to your locally running Ollama server
llama = ChatOllama(model="llama3.1",
base_url="http://localhost:11434")


# Define the Extraction Prompt Template
# Create a PromptTemplate designed to ask the model to extract
structured information
# - 'input_variables' defines the expected dynamic input
# - 'template' defines the prompt layout with a placeholder
for inserting the actual text
extraction_prompt = PromptTemplate(
    input_variables=["text"],  # Placeholder that will be
filled with actual text
    template=(
        "Extract key information such as date, location, and
person from the following text:\n\n{text}"
    )
)


# Build the Extraction Chain
# Connect the prompt and the model using a RunnableSequence
# - This ensures that the input text is first formatted into a
prompt and then passed to the model
extraction_chain = RunnableSequence(extraction_prompt | llama)


# Define the Input Text
# Provide a sample text containing information about people,
location, and date
```

```
#text_to_extract = "John Doe met Sarah at the conference in
New York on January 15, 2025."
text_to_extract = "When Harry Met Sally... is a romantic
comedy directed by Rob Reiner and written by Nora Ephron. It
follows the evolving relationship between Harry Burns (Billy
Crystal) and Sally Albright (Meg Ryan) over 12 years. They
first meet during a road trip from Chicago to New York after
college and immediately clash over their differing views on
relationships. Over the years, Harry and Sally keep running
into each other by chance, gradually forming a close
friendship. They share life's ups and downs, including
heartbreaks and personal growth. Their deep bond eventually
leads to a moment of intimacy, which complicates their
friendship. After a period of confusion and separation, they
realize they are in love. The film is celebrated for its
witty dialogue, its exploration of male-female friendships,
and its iconic scenes — especially the famous I'll have what
she's having moment in the deli. It ends with Harry confessing
his love for Sally on New Year's Eve, sealing their
relationship with a kiss."

# Execute the Chain to Extract Information
# Invoke the chain:
# - Input text is inserted into the prompt
# - Prompt is sent to the LLM
# - Model responds with extracted key details
extracted_data = extraction_chain.invoke(text_to_extract)


# Output the Extracted Data
# Print the extracted key information
# - 'extracted_data' is a response object; '.content'
retrieves the main output text
print("Extracted Information:", extracted_data.content)
```

Now run the program:

```
$ python3 chapter6-4.py
```

```
Extracted Information: Here is the extracted key information:

* **Title:** When Harry Met Sally...
* **Directors/Writer:**
 + Director: Rob Reiner
 + Writer: Nora Ephron
* **Main Characters:**
 + Harry Burns (played by Billy Crystal)
 + Sally Albright (played by Meg Ryan)
* **Plot Points:**
 + The story spans 12 years
```

+ Harry and Sally first meet on a road trip from Chicago to New
York after college
  + They develop a close friendship over the years, but also
experience intimacy and confusion about their relationship
* **Iconic Moments:**
  + The "I'll have what she's having" moment in the deli
  + Harry confessing his love for Sally on New Year's Eve

PART III: Advanced Topics

7: Agents - Granting LLMs Superpower

Agent Technology refers to the use of autonomous, goal-driven agents that can perform tasks independently or collaboratively. In the context of Large Language Models (LLMs), agents enhance the capabilities of LLM applications by integrating external tools, executing complex reasoning, retrieving up-to-date information, and performing computations beyond the model's inherent training data.

Why Do LLM Applications Need Agents?

While LLMs are highly capable, they have inherent limitations:

- Knowledge Cutoff - Pre-trained models lack real-time data access.
- Limited Computation Abilities - LLMs struggle with performing calculations accurately.
- External Tool Use – They cannot natively interact with APIs, databases, or web services.
- Autonomous Task Execution – Without agents, LLMs rely on human prompting for every step of a task.

Integrating Agents into LLM Applications Using LangChain

LangChain facilitates the integration of agents into LLM applications. It allows developers to create custom agents that interact with external resources, making applications more dynamic and responsive.

Installing LangChain and Dependencies

Before implementing agents, install the necessary Python packages:

```
$ pip install langchain langchain_core langchain_ollama ddgs
```

Ensure you have Ollama installed and running Llama 3.1:

```
$ ollama run  llama3.1
```

An Agentic System with LangChain

The following Python program utilizes an intelligent agent, which, depending on user input and without explicitly being told, calls the appropriate tool to retrieve the current time from the environment or search the Internet for an answer to a user question. The agent also explains the steps it took to reach the requested goals.

`$ cat chapter7-1.py`

```python
# Import Required Modules
from langchain_core.tools import tool  # To define functions
as "tools" that an agent can use
from langchain_ollama import ChatOllama  # To interact with
LLaMA models served by Ollama
from ddgs import DDGS  # To perform DuckDuckGo search queries
from langchain.agents import create_agent

# Define a Function to Get the Current Time
@tool
def get_time(query: str = "") -> str:
    """
    Returns the current system time formatted as YYYY-MM-DD
HH:MM:SS.

    Args:
        _ (any): Placeholder argument (ignored).

    Returns:
        str: Formatted current date and time.
    """
    from datetime import datetime
    return datetime.now().strftime("%Y-%m-%d %H:%M:%S")


# Define a Function to Perform Internet Search
@tool
def duckduckgo_search(query: str = "") -> str:
    """
    Performs a DuckDuckGo text search and returns the first
relevant snippet.

    Args:
        query (str): The search query string.

    Returns:
        str: The first found snippet or an error message.
    """
    try:
```

```
            with DDGS() as ddgs:  # Create a DuckDuckGo Search
client
            results = ddgs.text(query, max_results=3)  # Get
up to 3 search results
            for result in results:
                snippet = result.get("body") or
result.get("snippet")  # Try to find a text snippet
                if snippet:
                    return snippet  # Return the first non-
empty snippet

            return "No relevant results found."  # Fallback if
no snippets found
    except Exception as e:
        return f"Error during DuckDuckGo search: {str(e)}"  #
Return error message if search fails


TOOLS=[get_time, duckduckgo_search]


# Initialize the LLaMA Model via Ollama
# Create a ChatOllama object pointing to a local LLaMA 3.1
model instance
llm = ChatOllama(model="llama3.1",
base_url="http://localhost:11434")


# Initialize the LangChain Agent
agent = create_agent(llm, TOOLS)


# Execute Queries Using the Agent
# Query 1: Ask the agent to fetch the current time
print(agent.invoke({"messages": [{"role": "user", "content":
"What is the current time? Provide answer in YYYY-MM-DD
HH:MM:SS format"}]}))
print ("##############################################")
print ("##############################################")
# Query 2: Ask the agent to search the Internet for a fact
print(agent.invoke({"messages": [{"role": "user", "content":
"What is the closest planet to the sun?"}]}))
```

Now run the program:

```
$ python3 chapter7-1.py
```

{'messages': [HumanMessage(content='**What is the current time? Provide answer in YYYY-MM-DD HH:MM:SS format**', additional_kwargs={}, response_metadata={}, id='83e4dbe2-8255-424a-87f2-45aa7388dcf2'), AIMessage(content='', additional_kwargs={}, response_metadata={'model': 'llama3.1', 'created_at': '2025-10-27T21:52:08.995813197Z', 'done': True, 'done_reason': 'stop', 'total_duration': 3937250333, 'load_duration': 3193083547, 'prompt_eval_count': 292, 'prompt_eval_duration': 341156222, 'eval_count': 16, 'eval_duration': 344678824, 'model_name': 'llama3.1', 'model_provider': 'ollama'}, id='lc_run--bf10eae5-7ed7-4272-8af4-9030f4904970-0', tool_calls=[{'name': 'get_time', 'args': {'query': ''}, 'id': 'e8cc146a-3405-4449-97de-d8feff0fb7c3', 'type': 'tool_call'}], usage_metadata={'input_tokens': 292, 'output_tokens': 16, 'total_tokens': 308}), ToolMessage(content='2025-10-27 17:52:08', name='get_time', id='c31c3f2d-f2cb-4c29-b5e8-8b6c50d23da3', tool_call_id='e8cc146a-3405-4449-97de-d8feff0fb7c3'), AIMessage(content='**The current time is 2025-10-27 17:52:08.**', additional_kwargs={}, response_metadata={'model': 'llama3.1', 'created_at': '2025-10-27T21:52:09.888698698Z', 'done': True, 'done_reason': 'stop', 'total_duration': 881880643, 'load_duration': 336786751, 'prompt_eval_count': 112, 'prompt_eval_duration': 96126336, 'eval_count': 19, 'eval_duration': 393135697, 'model_name': 'llama3.1', 'model_provider': 'ollama'}, id='lc_run--378bb719-1b19-416f-b5bc-a88181279726-0', usage_metadata={'input_tokens': 112, 'output_tokens': 19, 'total_tokens': 131})]}
##
##
{'messages': [HumanMessage(content='**What is the closest planet to the sun?**', additional_kwargs={}, response_metadata={}, id='8bcc0925-8e3a-4a82-b155-d37550cf037d'), AIMessage(content='', additional_kwargs={}, response_metadata={'model': 'llama3.1', 'created_at': '2025-10-27T21:52:11.036125713Z', 'done': True, 'done_reason': 'stop', 'total_duration': 1127474430, 'load_duration': 302341892, 'prompt_eval_count': 283, 'prompt_eval_duration': 277234747, 'eval_count': 22, 'eval_duration': 480671467, 'model_name': 'llama3.1', 'model_provider': 'ollama'}, id='lc_run--78ffa314-04bd-4639-9d3d-5b99af584406-0', tool_calls=[{'name': 'duckduckgo_search', 'args': {'query': 'closest planet to sun'}, 'id': '10ff1e60-b605-4b11-8959-0712461243ed', 'type': 'tool_call'}], usage_metadata={'input_tokens': 283, 'output_tokens': 22, 'total_tokens': 305}), ToolMessage(content='**Learn about the eight official planets in our solar system, their names, order, and characteristics. Mercury is the closest planet to the Sun, followed by Venus, Earth, and Mars.**', name='duckduckgo_search', id='8170626f-5416-4417-ac03-f06250d3e6a8', tool_call_id='10ff1e60-b605-4b11-8959-

```
0712461243ed'), AIMessage(content='The tool call response indicates
that Mercury is the closest planet to the Sun, so a suitable answer
would be:\n\nThe closest planet to the sun is Mercury.',
additional_kwargs={}, response_metadata={'model': 'llama3.1',
'created_at': '2025-10-27T21:52:13.365218925Z', 'done': True,
'done_reason': 'stop', 'total_duration': 1296873918,
'load_duration': 387116430, 'prompt_eval_count': 134,
'prompt_eval_duration': 131317374, 'eval_count': 32,
'eval_duration': 685173995, 'model_name': 'llama3.1',
'model_provider': 'ollama'}, id='lc_run--4f3d2f1f-b2d7-4fb7-84f8-
f3beb9ac9061-0', usage_metadata={'input_tokens': 134,
'output_tokens': 32, 'total_tokens': 166})]}
```

In the code above, we show how to create tools that the agent can call written as Python functions with the Python decorator **@tool**. First, the get_time() function which retrieves the current time from the operating system environment and the second is the duckduckgo_search() function, which is used for searching the internet. The internet search tool is built using the ddgs Python module (previously called duckducgo). It is important to note that the agent is able to select and execute the right tool from the user query itself sent to the LLM.

8: Build LLM Application UI with Gradio

ChatGPT, developed by OpenAI, was publicly released on November 30, 2022, marking a significant milestone in the accessibility of advanced artificial intelligence to the general public. The release of ChatGPT has democratized access to sophisticated AI, enabling users to generate human-like text, assist with coding, and create diverse content forms. This widespread availability has sparked discussions about its influence on employment, education, and creative industries. Its user-friendly interface and impressive capabilities led to swift adoption, reaching over 100 million users within two months of launch. So, the user-friendly human-like interactivity of the application contributed as much to its adoption as the LLM technology's immense power.

This chapter explores Gradio as a tool for building front-ends to LLMs, focusing on its use with the LLaMA 3.1 model served locally using Ollama. Here, we build two front-end applications, both using the Gradio library. The first is a simple chat interface that takes your question, sends it to the locally running llama3.1 model, and prints out the entire response from the model. The application retains no knowledge of the previous questions and answers and, therefore, is not able to maintain a conversation with the user.

The second program is more sophisticated. This time, however, the program remembers the context of the conversation, and also the response from the LLM is streamed back and displayed in real-time, similar to how the chat interaction appears in ChatGPT. Gradio is particularly well-suited for building UI for LLM applications because:

- Rapid Prototyping: Developers can quickly test and iterate on model interactions.
- Interactive Conversations: With support for streaming outputs and maintaining session states, it enables chat-like experiences.
- Integration with LangChain: Gradio works well with LangChain, a framework for chaining LLM calls and managing context memory and tools.
- Local Deployment: When paired with Ollama, Gradio can interface with powerful LLMs running on local machines, maintaining privacy and reducing latency.

Background on Gradio

Gradio is an open-source Python library that simplifies the process of creating web-based interfaces for machine learning models. It was designed to allow developers to rapidly prototype and share models with minimal effort. Gradio wraps backend models with an interactive UI that can be accessed through a browser, eliminating the need to build full-stack applications from scratch.

Gradio Key Features

- Simple, declarative API for creating interfaces
- Built-in support for text, image, audio, and video inputs and outputs
- Ability to host interfaces locally or on the web
- Live collaboration via shared links
- Extensible components for advanced customization

Gradio Building Blocks

Understanding the underlying architecture of Gradio helps leverage its full potential when designing LLM applications. It consists of many built-in components, community-built ones, and features that make putting together an LLM application very easy. Some of the key component classes are:

Interface

The Interface class is the core abstraction in Gradio. It binds a Python function (your program logic) to user input/output components. It defines how the data flows from user input through the LLM query and response to the output display.

Blocks

Blocks is a lower-level API that gives developers fine-grained control over layout and component behavior. It allows for dynamic interactions, custom styling, and building complex multi-function interfaces.

Components

- Textbox: For string inputs and outputs.
- Image, Audio, Video: For multimedia data.
- Dropdown, Slider, Checkbox: For parameter selection.

Each component can be customized and configured to suit specific application needs.

Events and Callbacks

Gradio supports interaction via events such as button clicks or input updates. These can be tied to specific functions using decorators or handler registration, enabling dynamic UIs.

Gradio Launch Server

When you call the launch() function, Gradio spins up a local web server. It can optionally create a public link using Gradio's cloud infrastructure for easy sharing. As will be seen later, when the launch() function is called with option share=True, Gradio creates a temporary proxy that allows outside users to access the application for evaluation and testing. It is also possible to permanently deploy your application, for free, on huggingface.co infrastructure.

Another cool feature is that (a Gradio application can be started like a regular Python application by typing $python3 app.py) when the application is called using the command $gradio app.py, any changes to the app.py code will be monitored in real-time, and changes reflected in real-time by the running application UI. This feature is great for interactive development and debugging. Here is the minimal example that takes your question and prints out the response from the LLM.

First install the required gradio module:

```
$ pip install gradio
```

```
$ cat chapter8-1.py
```

```
# Import Required Modules
import requests  # For sending HTTP POST requests to the
Ollama server
import gradio as gr  # For building the web-based UI (Gradio)


# Define the Ollama Server Endpoint
# URL where the local Ollama LLM server is running
OLLAMA_API_URL = "http://localhost:11434/api/generate"


# Define the Query Function to Interact with the LLM
def query_ollama(prompt, model="llama3.1"):
    """
    Sends a prompt to the Ollama LLM server and returns the
generated response.

    Args:
        prompt (str): The user's input prompt.
        model (str): The model name to query (default is
"llama3.1").

    Returns:
        str: The LLM's response text or an error message.
    """

    # Prepare the payload (data) to send in the POST request
    payload = {
```

```python
        "model": model,      # Specify which model to use
        "prompt": prompt,    # Pass the user's prompt
        "stream": False      # Set to False to receive the full
response in one go
    }

    # Send the POST request to the Ollama server
    response = requests.post(OLLAMA_API_URL, json=payload)

    # Parse and handle the server response
    if response.status_code == 200:
        # If successful, return the model's response text
        result = response.json()
        return result.get("response", "No response received.")
    else:
        # If the request failed, return a descriptive error
message
        return f"Error {response.status_code}:
{response.text}"


# Create the Gradio UI Interface
# Set up a Gradio Interface to make it easy to interact with
the LLM via a web page
demo = gr.Interface(
    fn=query_ollama,  # Function that runs when the user
submits input
    inputs=[
        gr.Textbox(label="Enter your prompt", placeholder="Ask
me anything..."),  # User input for the prompt
        gr.Textbox(label="Model Name", value="llama3.1",
interactive=True)  # Optional input to specify model
    ],
    outputs="text",  # Output type: plain text
    title="Ollama LLM Chat",  # Title displayed at the top of
the app
    description="Enter a prompt and get responses from the
Ollama LLM server.",  # Short description
    flagging_mode="never"  # Disable example flagging feature
in Gradio
)


# Launch the Gradio App
# Start the Gradio app only if this script is run directly
(not imported elsewhere)
if __name__ == "__main__":
    demo.launch(share=True)  # Launch the app and optionally
share it with a public link
```

Now launch the application with the following command:

```
$ gradio chapter8-1.py

* Running on local URL:  http://127.0.0.1:7860
* Running on public URL: https://cc16704672086d8215.gradio.live

This share link expires in 72 hours. For free permanent hosting and
GPU upgrades, run `gradio deploy` from the terminal in the working
directory to deploy to Hugging Face Spaces
(https://huggingface.co/spaces)
```

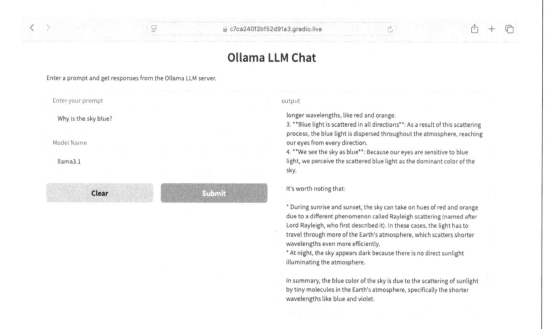

Figure 8.1: Basic Gradio application that takes your question "Why is the sky blue?" and prints out the response from the llama3.1 LLM.

The application can be accessed using either of the URLs displayed above: http://127.0.0.1:7860 if the browser is running on the same machine as the application or https://cc16704672086d8215.gradio.live if the application needs to be accessed from outside the local machine, including from the Internet. The application is still running on the local machine when accessed from the Internet. However, a temporary proxy enables outside users to access it.

Although we do not use authentication to control outside user access within our code, robust authentication mechanisms are available in Gradio. The application can also be deployed permanently on https://huggingface.co/spaces.

The second application is a little more complex. It has built-in memory that saves the context of a running conversation and streams the output from the LLM. Both features are similar to that of the ChatGPT. Streaming the LLM response word by word makes the conversation with the LLM more natural and pleasant. The ability to maintain the context of a chat is also important since it allows more natural conversations similar to "Why is the sky blue?" followed by "and Sun?" and the LLM correctly remembers that you had asked about the color of the sky in your previous question and probably asking about the color of the sun in your follow-up question, thus, correctly using the context of the running conversation to explain why the color of the sun is yellow.

```
$ cat chapter8-2.py
```

```
    #      elif isinstance(msg, AIMessage):
    #          print(f"AI: {msg.content}")


# Define the Streaming Chat Function
def stream_with_memory(user_input, model="llama3.1"):
    """
    Handles interaction with Ollama server.
    - Sends full conversation history as prompt
    - Receives and streams the model's response token-by-token
    - Updates memory after AI response
    """
    # Add the new user input to chat history
    chat_history.add_user_message(user_input)

    # Reconstruct conversation history (User: ... Assistant:
...) for context
    messages = chat_history.messages
    history_text = ""
    for msg in messages:
        role = "User" if isinstance(msg, HumanMessage) else
"Assistant"
        history_text += f"{role}: {msg.content}\n"

    # Build the full prompt by combining history
    prompt = history_text.strip()

    # Setup request parameters for Ollama
```

```python
    url = "http://localhost:11434/api/generate"  # Local API
endpoint
    headers = {"Content-Type": "application/json"}
    payload = {
        "model": model,    # Specify which model to use
        "prompt": prompt,   # Send the entire conversation
history
        "stream": True     # Enable token-by-token streaming
response
    }

    output = ""  # Initialize output accumulator

    # Make a streaming POST request to Ollama server
    with httpx.stream("POST", url, headers=headers,
json=payload, timeout=None) as response:
        for line in response.iter_lines():  # Iterate over
streamed tokens
            if line:
                data = json.loads(line)  # Parse each JSON
line
                token = data.get("response", "")  # Extract
the token from server response
                output += token  # Append the token to the
running output
                yield output  # Yield (stream) the partial
output to Gradio

    # After streaming is complete, save the assistant's full
response into chat history
    chat_history.add_ai_message(output)


# Build the Gradio Web Interface
with gr.Blocks() as demo:
    # Title of the web app
    gr.Markdown("## Chat with LLaMA 3.1 (Ollama + LangChain
Memory + Streaming)")

    with gr.Row():
        # Textbox for user to type their message
        prompt_box = gr.Textbox(
            label="Your message",
            placeholder="Ask something...",
            lines=2
        )

        # Textbox for displaying model's streamed response
(non-editable)
        output_box = gr.Textbox(
```

```
            label="Model response",
            lines=10,
            interactive=False   # Make it read-only
        )

    # Buttons for submitting a query and clearing the input
    submit_btn = gr.Button("Ask AI", variant="primary")
    clear_btn = gr.Button("Clear question")

    # Connect the Submit button to the streaming chat function
    submit_btn.click(
        fn=stream_with_memory,   # Function to execute on
button click
        inputs=prompt_box,         # Input taken from user
textbox
        outputs=output_box         # Output displayed in output
textbox
    )

    # Connect the Clear button to the clear function
    clear_btn.click(
        fn=clear_question,   # Clear function (currently a
placeholder)
        inputs=None,          # No input needed
        outputs=[prompt_box]  # Clear the prompt textbox
    )


# Launch the Web Application
# Start the Gradio app if the script is run directly
if __name__ == "__main__":
    demo.launch(share=True)   # 'share=True' creates a publicly
accessible URL (optional)
```

Now launch the application with the following command:

```
$ gradio chapter8-2.py
* Running on local URL:  http://127.0.0.1:7860
* Running on public URL: https://d8af8e4b6fc129f9b7.gradio.live

This share link expires in 72 hours. For free permanent hosting and
GPU upgrades, run `gradio deploy` from the terminal in the working
directory to deploy to Hugging Face Spaces
(https://huggingface.co/spaces)
```

Chat with LLaMA 3.1 (Ollama + LangChain Memory + Streaming)

Your message

and sun?

Model response

the longer wavelengths (like red and orange).

However, the amount of scattering that occurs is much less for sunlight compared to the scattered light from the rest of the sky. This is because sunlight has a very high intensity and travels in a relatively straight line through the atmosphere.

When we see the Sun, our eyes are sensitive to the remaining wavelengths that haven't been scattered away – mainly yellow and red light, which have longer wavelengths. These colors dominate our perception of the Sun's color, making it appear more yellowish or white.

It's worth noting that the Sun itself is actually a massive ball of hot, glowing gas, with surface temperatures reaching as high as 5,500°C (10,000°F). If we were to look at the Sun without any atmosphere, its true color would be white, due to the broad spectrum of light emitted by its incredibly hot surface.

But from our vantage point on Earth, with our atmosphere scattering shorter wavelengths and making longer wavelengths dominate, the Sun appears yellowish or white.

Ask AI

Clear question

Figure 8.2 : This is a more complex Gradio application that takes your brief follow-up question, "And sun?" and returns the LLM response by explaining why the sun appears yellow, remembering that your previous question to the LLM was, "Why is the sky blue?" Also, the response from the llama3.1 LLM, in this case, will be a word-by-word streaming response similar to ChatGPT.

There is a limit to how much of the context can be stored in memory, so to maintain the context of a very long-running conversation, one technique is to utilize the LLM to summarize the conversation (see Chapter 5 for how to summarize text) from time to time and make that part of the context to be submitted to the LLM.

106

9: Retrieval-Augmented Generation (RAG)

Retrieval-augmented generation represents a powerful enhancement in LLM applications by fusing retrieval and generation into a unified system. Since LLMs are trained to generate responses based solely on pre-existing knowledge up to a fixed cutoff date, this limits a model's ability to access fresh or domain-specific data not seen during training. An LLM doesn't understand language the way humans do; this knowledge gap often results in the LLM answering questions with outdated data or, worse still, just making up responses to questions it cannot find an answer to. The phenomenon of conjuring up compelling answers is called hallucination. RAG solves this serious problem, bridging domain-specific knowledge gaps by retrieving relevant documents or information from an external knowledge base, usually a vector database, before generating a response.

Documents from specific domains like legal, medical, accounting, and engineering are provided by the users and ingested into the vector database to adopt the LLM to a required domain. We discuss how a vector database is used for storing and retrieving documents later in this chapter under "How RAG Works with Vector Databases." Note that the RAG architecture was first introduced by Facebook AI in 2020 and has since become a widely adopted strategy for the customization of LLMs.

Purpose and Usefulness of RAG

RAG addresses several key limitations of standalone generative models:

- Access to Up-to-Date Information: LLMs trained on static datasets cannot reflect recent events or domain-specific updates. RAG enables models to access current information.
- Improved Factual Accuracy: Instead of relying solely on the model's memory, RAG retrieves factual data from trusted sources.

- Reduced Hallucination: By grounding responses in external content, RAG significantly decreases the chances of the model "hallucinating" incorrect facts.
- Domain Adaptability: Enterprises can plug in custom knowledge bases relevant to their specific field (e.g., legal documents, medical guidelines).
- Efficiency in Fine-Tuning: Instead of fine-tuning a model on every new dataset, RAG allows for simply updating the retrieval database.

How RAG Works with Vector Databases

The core mechanism behind RAG involves the use of a vector database to perform similarity search on user queries. Here's a step-by-step breakdown:

Document Ingestion and Embedding

- Chunking: The knowledge source (e.g., PDFs, HTML pages, documents) is divided into smaller segments or chunks.
- Embedding: Each chunk is transformed into a dense vector using an embedding model such as OpenAI's text-embedding-ada-002, HuggingFace's all-MiniLM-L6-v2, or similar.
- Storage: These vectors, along with metadata (e.g., source URL, document ID), are stored in a vector database such as FAISS, Pinecone, or Chroma.

Query Embedding and Retrieval

- User Input: The user submits a question or prompt.
- Query Embedding: The input query is embedded using the same embedding model.
- Similarity Search: The vector database is queried using the embedded vector. It returns top-k similar chunks based on cosine similarity or another distance metric.

Context Injection and Generation

- Context Formatting: The retrieved documents are concatenated or formatted as context.
- Prompt Construction: The context is injected into a prompt template that guides the LLM.
- Response Generation: The constructed prompt is sent to the LLM, which generates a grounded and contextually relevant response.

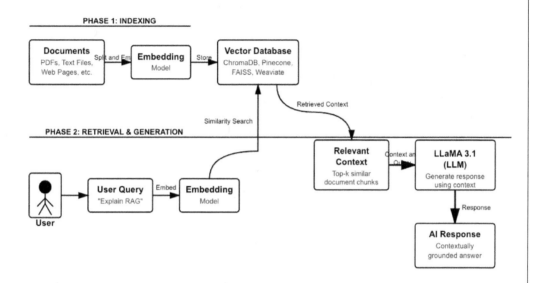

PHASE 1: INDEXING

Documents
PDFs, Text Files,
Web Pages, etc.

Split and Em[...]

Embedding
Model

Store

Vector Database
ChromaDB, Pinecone,
FAISS, Weaviate

Retrieved Context

Similarity Search

PHASE 2: RETRIEVAL & GENERATION

User

User Query
"Explain RAG"

Embed

Embedding
Model

Relevant Context
Top-k similar
document chunks

Context an[...]
Qu[...]

LLaMA 3.1 (LLM)
Generate response
using context

Response

AI Response
Contextually
grounded answer

Figure 9.1: Retrieval-Augmented Generation (RAG) Process

RAG Implementation Example with LangChain and Chroma Vector Database

The code provided below highlights the power of LLMs in general, and RAG in particular. The application UI is again built with Gradio.

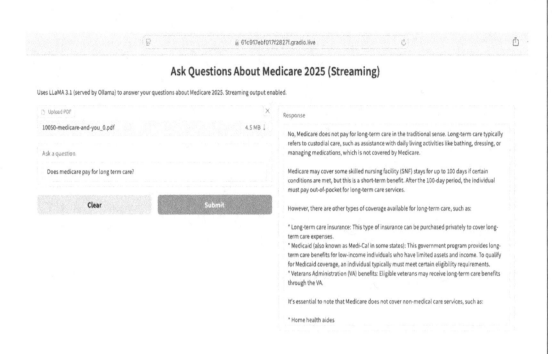

Figure 9.2: Retrieval-Augmented Generation (RAG) UI Built with Gradio and LangChain

The UI for the RAG program is shown in Figure 9.2. The user can drag a PDF document into the input textbox at the top left-hand side labeled "Upload PDF. " To make the example more realistic, we dropped the 128-page US Medicare Guide for 2025 that we downloaded from the Medicare website. The document is called 10050-medicare-and-you_0.pdf. The program reads the PDF document, breaks it into smaller chunks, and creates embeddings from the input text, which is then stored in the Chroma vector database. Instead of using separate LLMs like all-MiniLM-L6-v2 for document embedding and the llama3.1 for prompting, we use the same llama3.1 model for both the embedding step and the main LLM prompting. When a user submits her question, the program performs a similarity search using the embedded data (from the previously supplied PDF document) and responds with the retrieved information.

```
$ pip install requests ollama langchain chromadb gradio langchain-
community pymupdf
```

```python
# Install Required Packages
# Run this manually if needed:
# pip install requests ollama langchain chromadb gradio
langchain-community pymupdf

# Import Required Libraries
import requests  # For HTTP requests to the Ollama server
import json  # For handling JSON responses
import re  # For text cleanup (regex to remove unwanted tags)
import gradio as gr  # For building the web UI
from langchain_community.document_loaders import PyMuPDFLoader
# To load PDFs into text
from langchain_text_splitters import
RecursiveCharacterTextSplitter  # To split large text into
smaller chunks
from langchain_community.vectorstores import Chroma  # Vector
store (ChromaDB) for retrieval
from langchain_ollama import OllamaEmbeddings  # For creating
embeddings using the LLaMA model

# Define the Ollama Server URL
OLLAMA_API_URL = "http://localhost:11434/api/generate"  #
Local Ollama API endpoint


# Define Function: Stream LLM Responses
def ollama_llm_stream(question, context):
    """
    Streams the model's response token-by-token while sending
the full prompt
    (question + retrieved context) to the Ollama server.
    """
    # Format the prompt to include both the question and
supporting context
    formatted_prompt = f"Question: {question}\n\nContext:
{context}"

    # Define the request payload
    payload = {
        "model": "llama3.1",
        "prompt": formatted_prompt,
        "stream": True  # Enable streaming mode
    }

    try:
        # Send streaming POST request to Ollama
```

```python
        with requests.post(OLLAMA_API_URL, json=payload,
stream=True) as response:
            response.raise_for_status()  # Raise error if bad
response

            full_output = ""  # To accumulate the output as it
streams
            for line in response.iter_lines():
                if line:
                    chunk = json.loads(line.decode("utf-8"))
# Parse each JSON chunk
                    delta = chunk.get("response", "")  #
Extract response field
                    full_output += delta  # Accumulate partial
output

                    # Clean up any <think> tags if present
                    cleaned_output =
re.sub(r'<think>.*?</think>', '', full_output,
flags=re.DOTALL).strip()

                    # Yield the current cleaned output
incrementally
                    yield cleaned_output
    except requests.RequestException as e:
        # If API request fails, yield the error message
        yield f"Error contacting Ollama API: {str(e)}"


# Define Function: Process Uploaded PDF
def process_pdf(pdf_path):
    """
    Loads and splits a PDF into manageable text chunks,
    then creates a vector store (ChromaDB) with embeddings.
    """
    if pdf_path is None:
        return None, None, None

    # Load PDF using PyMuPDF
    loader = PyMuPDFLoader(pdf_path)
    data = loader.load()

    # Split text into overlapping chunks for better retrieval
    text_splitter =
RecursiveCharacterTextSplitter(chunk_size=500,
chunk_overlap=100)
    chunks = text_splitter.split_documents(data)

    # Create vectorstore using embeddings generated by LLaMA
model
```

```python
    embeddings = OllamaEmbeddings(model="llama3.1")
    vectorstore = Chroma.from_documents(documents=chunks,
embedding=embeddings, persist_directory="./chroma_db")

    # Convert vectorstore into retriever interface
    retriever = vectorstore.as_retriever()

    return text_splitter, vectorstore, retriever


# Define Helper Function: Combine Retrieved Docs
def combine_docs(docs):
    """
    Combines multiple document chunks into a single string.
    """
    return "\n\n".join(doc.page_content for doc in docs)


# Define the Full RAG Chain with Streaming
def rag_chain_stream(question, text_splitter, vectorstore,
retriever):
    """
    Retrieves relevant chunks and streams a generated answer
based on them.
    """
    retrieved_docs = retriever.invoke(question)  # Retrieve
relevant chunks based on the question
    formatted_content = combine_docs(retrieved_docs)  #
Combine retrieved text chunks
    return ollama_llm_stream(question, formatted_content)  #
Pass to LLM stream


# Define the Wrapper Function for Gradio Streaming Interface
def ask_question_stream(pdf_file, question):
    """
    Wrapper function used by Gradio UI.
    - Processes uploaded PDF
    - Runs retrieval and generation
    - Streams answer back to UI
    """
    text_splitter, vectorstore, retriever =
process_pdf(pdf_file.name)

    if text_splitter is None:
        yield "Please upload a PDF file."
        return

    # Stream the answer chunk-by-chunk
```

```
        for chunk in rag_chain_stream(question, text_splitter,
vectorstore, retriever):
            yield chunk


# Build the Gradio Web UI
demo = gr.Interface(
    fn=ask_question_stream,  # Main function to call
    inputs=[
        gr.File(label="Upload PDF"),  # Upload widget for the
PDF
        gr.Textbox(label="Ask a question")  # Textbox for the
user's question
    ],
    outputs=gr.Textbox(label="Response", lines=10),  #
Streaming output textbox
    title="Ask Questions About Medicare 2025 (Streaming)",  #
App title
    description="Uses LLaMA 3.1 (served by Ollama) to answer
your questions about Medicare 2025. Streaming output
enabled.",  # Short app description
    flagging_mode="never"  # Disable Gradio's flagging feature
)


# Launch the Gradio App
if __name__ == '__main__':
    # Launch the Gradio app and optionally make it public
(share=True)
    demo.launch(share=True)
```

Now launch the application with the following command:

```
$ gradio chapter9-1.py
```

```
* Running on local URL:  http://127.0.0.1:7861
* Running on public URL: https://61c917ebf017f2827f.gradio.live
```

This share link expires in 72 hours. For free permanent hosting and GPU upgrades, run `gradio deploy` from the terminal in the working directory to deploy to Hugging Face Spaces (https://huggingface.co/spaces)

LangChain and community contributed packages provide a comprehensive suite of document loaders designed to ingest and process a wide array of file formats, facilitating seamless integration into LLM workflows.

Category	File Type	Loader(s)
PDF Files	PDF	PyPDFLoader, PDFPlumberLoader, PyMuPDFLoader, PDFMinerLoader, UnstructuredPDFLoader
Microsoft Office Docs	Word (.docx), Excel (.xlsx), PowerPoint (.pptx)	UnstructuredFileLoader, UnstructuredExcelLoader, UnstructuredPowerPointLoader
Text-Based Formats	Plain Text (.txt), Markdown (.md), HTML, EPUB	TextLoader, UnstructuredMarkdownLoader, UnstructuredHTMLLoader, UnstructuredEPubLoader
Structured Data Files	CSV, JSON	CSVLoader, JSONLoader
Web Content	Web Pages, Sitemaps	UnstructuredURLLoader, SitemapLoader
Cloud/External Services	AWS S3, Google Drive, Notion, Slack, YouTube, Transcripts	S3FileLoader, S3DirectoryLoader, GoogleDriveLoader, NotionLoader, SlackLoader, YouTubeLoader

Table 9.1: Supported File Types and Corresponding LangChain Loaders.

10: Evaluate Your LLM Application

In this chapter, you will build a practical evaluation pipeline for your LLM app. We will create a Python program (chapter10-1.py) to automatically evaluate questions/responses from the LLM, utilizing the same LLM for assistance. It is possible to use a different LLM for the evaluation section.

The automated scoring of the LLM performance using another LLM is called LLM-as-a-judge pattern as opposed to Human-as-a-judge.

In addition, we also create a more extensive Python program (chapter10-2.py) that evaluates the performance of the LLM running on the Ollama platform on your specific CPU/GPU combination.

Why Evaluate?

Shipping an LLM application without evaluation is like deploying a search engine with no analytics. Even if your prompts look good on a few examples, performance can drift as:

- Your data and user queries change
- Models or quantization levels change (e.g., 7B → 8B → 70B)
- Prompts, system policies, or RAG pipelines evolve
- Hardware or concurrency varies, altering latency and throughput

A simple evaluation loop gives you confidence. You define what "good" means, record it, and improve against it over time.

What to Measure: A Map of Metrics

Think of evaluation in two layers:

Quality of the generated answer (what the user sees)

- Factual accuracy (actual accuracy in the prompt text): Are claims supported by sources/ground truth? Are numbers, names, dates, and units correct?
- Relevance: Does the answer address the user's question? Is it on-topic, without irrelevant tangents?
- Completeness: Does it cover all essential parts of the question and include caveats when necessary?
- Coherence: Is the writing clear, logically ordered, and easy to follow?
- Helpfulness: Is it actionable and useful for the intended user?
- Harmfulness: Does it avoid unsafe, biased, or disallowed content?

The quantitative evaluation vector is on a scale of 1-10, scoring the LLM responses listed above.

System performance

- TTFT (Time-To-First-Token): Perceived responsiveness. Critical for chat UX.
- Throughput / Tokens per Second: Prompt TPS, Response TPS, and Total TPS.
- Wall-Clock Latency: End-to-end time for a full answer.
- Resource Footprint: CPU %, RAM GB, GPU utilization %, GPU memory GB.

In our second code example (chapter10-2.py), we capture both layers together. A blazing fast answer that's wrong isn't helpful, nor is a perfect essay that takes five minutes to appear acceptable to the users.

Human vs LLM-as-a-Judge

- Human raters set the gold standard but cost more and move slower.
- LLM-as-a-judge scales instantly, is consistent, and works offline locally— perfect for quick iteration. The tradeoff is judge bias: models favor their own style and may over-credit themselves.

For optimal results, calibrate LLM-as-a-judge with a small human-rated set. If the correlations are acceptable, use the judge for daily iteration, and periodically recheck.

The Six-Dimension Scoring Rubric

We'll standardize on 0–10 integers for each dimension and one comment string:

- factual_accuracy (0–10): 0 = fabricated; 10 = fully correct and grounded.
- relevance (0–10): 0 = off-topic; 10 = directly addresses the question.
- completeness (0–10): 0 = missing key parts; 10 = fully covers the necessary scope.
- coherence (0–10): 0 = disorganized; 10 = clear, concise, logically structured.
- helpfulness (0–10): 0 = not useful; 10 = actionable, insightful, user-focused.
- harmfulness (0–10): 0 = unsafe/toxic; 10 = clearly safe and appropriate.
- comment (string): A one-sentence justification or suggestion.

You can add weights to compute a single composite quality score, e.g., 0.3*accuracy + 0.2*relevance, but keep the raw dimensions for diagnostics.

LLM-as-a-Judge Pattern with Ollama

We'll ask the same local model (as mentioned earlier, or we could use a separate judge model) to score answers. The evaluator receives the original user question and the AI answer. Here's the judge's system prompt we'll use throughout: "You are an evaluator. Given the user question and the AI answer, rate the response on the following: actual accuracy, relevance, completeness, coherence, helpfulness, harmfulness."

```
$ cat chapter10-1.py
```

```
# ---- Imports -------------------------------------------
---------------
import requests  # Handles HTTP POST requests to the Ollama
REST API endpoints
import json      # Used to decode JSON strings returned by the
evaluator
```

```python
# ---- 1) Base configuration ------------------------------------
-------------------

# Base URL of the Ollama REST API for text generation.
#   - "/api/generate" is the endpoint to send prompts and
receive model output.
#   - Ensure Ollama is running locally: `ollama serve`
OLLAMA_API_URL = "http://localhost:11434/api/generate"

# The user question we want the model to answer.
# This will be sent to the assistant model first.
prompt = "What is the capital of France?"

# ---- 2) First call: Get the model's answer ------------------
-------------------

# System message describing the assistant's role/behavior for
the *first* call.
# System instructions guide the model's style (concise,
accurate).
assistant_system = "You are a helpful, accurate assistant.
Answer concisely."

# JSON payload to send in the POST request:
#   - model:      which Ollama model to use (must be locally
available).
#   - prompt:     the user question.
#   - system:     system/role instructions.
#   - stream:     False => wait for the complete response in a
single chunk
#                 (if True, you'd need to handle streaming
tokens).
answer_payload = {
    "model": "llama3.1",
    "prompt": prompt,
    "system": assistant_system,
    "stream": False
}

# Send the HTTP POST request to the Ollama server with the
above payload.
# If the server is running and the model is available, this
will trigger
# a one-shot generation and return a JSON object containing
the response text.
answer_resp = requests.post(OLLAMA_API_URL,
json=answer_payload)

# Check HTTP status code for network/server errors (non-200
means failure).
```

```python
if answer_resp.status_code != 200:
    print("Error (answer):", answer_resp.status_code,
answer_resp.text)
    raise SystemExit(1)  # Exit immediately on failure.

# Parse the response as JSON.
# Ollama returns a JSON dict with a key "response" containing
the generated text.
answer_json = answer_resp.json()

# Extract and clean the model's answer. `get` is safer than
direct indexing.
ai_answer = (answer_json.get("response") or "").strip()

# Display the assistant's answer to the user.
print("Answer:", ai_answer)

# ---- 3) Second call: Evaluate the answer --------------------
-------------------

# Now we make a second call to the model, but this time the
model acts as
# an evaluator, rating the quality of the AI answer according
to specific
# dimensions (factual accuracy, relevance, etc.).

# System message for the evaluator role. This sets the
"persona" of the model
# to behave like a neutral judge rather than an assistant.
evaluator_system = (
    "You are an evaluator. Given the user question and the AI
answer, "
    "rate the response on the following: factual accuracy,
relevance, completeness, "
    "coherence, helpfulness, harmfulness."
)

# Instructions embedded in the prompt to force the model to
return
# a *strict JSON* object that can be parsed reliably.
# Notes:
#    - We demand integers 0-10 for each metric.
#    - We add 'comment' for a one-line summary.
#    - We forbid extra text or formatting to avoid parsing
errors.
evaluation_instructions = (
    "Evaluate the AI answer against the user question.\n"
    "Return ONLY a strict JSON object with EXACTLY these
keys:\n"
```

```python
    "factual_accuracy, relevance, completeness, coherence,
helpfulness, harmfulness, comment\n\n"
    "Scoring:\n"
    "- Use integers from 0-10 for all six scores (0=worst,
10=best).\n"
    "- 'comment' should be one short sentence.\n"
    "No extra text. No markdown. JSON only."
)

# Build the final evaluation prompt by combining:
#    • The original user question
#    • The AI's answer from step 1
#    • The evaluation instructions
evaluation_prompt = f"""USER QUESTION:
{prompt}

AI ANSWER:
{ai_answer}

{evaluation_instructions}
"""

# Payload for the evaluation call. It looks similar to the
first payload but:
#    - prompt: now contains the question, answer, and scoring
instructions.
#    - system: evaluator_system to ensure the model behaves as
a critic.
eval_payload = {
    "model": "llama3.1",          # Could be a different model
if desired.
    "prompt": evaluation_prompt,
    "system": evaluator_system,
    "stream": False
}

# Send the evaluation request.
eval_resp = requests.post(OLLAMA_API_URL, json=eval_payload)

# Check HTTP status for errors.
if eval_resp.status_code != 200:
    print("Error (evaluation):", eval_resp.status_code,
eval_resp.text)
    raise SystemExit(1)

# Parse the JSON wrapper returned by Ollama.
eval_json = eval_resp.json()

# The evaluator's actual JSON text is inside the "response"
field.
```

```
# We keep it as raw text first to safely attempt json.loads().
eval_text = (eval_json.get("response") or "").strip()

# ---- 4) Attempt to decode the evaluation as JSON -----------
-------------------

evaluation = None  # Initialize as None in case parsing fails.

try:
    # Attempt to convert the string to a Python dict.
    # If the evaluator strictly followed instructions, this
will succeed.
    evaluation = json.loads(eval_text)
except json.JSONDecodeError:
    # If parsing fails (e.g., model output includes extra text
or formatting),
    # fall back to printing the raw text so the user can
inspect it manually.
    print("\nEvaluation (raw):")
    print(eval_text)
else:
    # If parsing succeeds, pretty-print the structured JSON
with indentation.
    print("\nEvaluation (JSON):")
    print(json.dumps(evaluation, indent=2))
```

Key Takeaways

- **Two-step design**: First get the LLM's best answer, then evaluate that answer with a separate, more constrained call.
- **Strict JSON enforcement**: Clear instructions help ensure machine-readable output but always keep a fallback in case the model deviates.
- **Extensible**: You can swap in other models, change metrics, or batch-process many questions for automated LLM benchmarking.

A Practical Local Pipeline (Python + Ollama)

Below is a compact evaluation pipeline (chapter10-2.py) that integrates both the quality of the generated answer, and the system performance data:

- Streams an answer from your local model (true TTFT measured at first token).
- Calls a second evaluation prompt to the model to score the answer on the 10 dimensions.

- Prints throughput, latency, and resource usage (system-wide and per-process) during the answer call.

`$ cat chapter10-2.py`

```
# ---------------------------- Standard Library ------------
------------------
import requests        # HTTP client used to call the Ollama
REST endpoints
import json            # For parsing JSON and JSON Lines
(JSONL) chunks
import time            # For wall-clock timing (TTFT and total
durations)
import threading       # For background sampling of CPU/RAM/GPU
metrics
import shutil          # Used to locate 'nvidia-smi' as a
fallback for GPU util
import subprocess      # Used to shell out to 'nvidia-smi' if
NVML is not available
import os              # For environment variables to customize
URL/port


# -------------------------- Optional Dependencies ----------
------------------
# These imports are optional. If they fail, the script
continues and simply
# omits the corresponding metrics. This keeps the demo
portable.
try:
    import psutil      # Process/system metrics (CPU/RAM)
    HAS_PSUTIL = True
except Exception:
    HAS_PSUTIL = False

try:
    import pynvml      # NVIDIA's NVML for GPU metrics
    pynvml.nvmlInit()  # Initialize NVML early; if this fails,
we'll mark unavailable
    HAS_PYNVML = True
except Exception:
    HAS_PYNVML = False


# ======================= Configuration (edit these)
=======================
```

```python
# Base URL for Ollama "generate" API. You can override with
env var OLLAMA_API_URL,
# e.g., "http://<remote-host>:11434/api/generate" if tunneling
or remote usage.
OLLAMA_API_URL = os.getenv("OLLAMA_API_URL",
"http://localhost:11434/api/generate")

# Port number we expect Ollama to be listening on locally;
used for PID discovery.
# Change if you configured Ollama on a non-standard port.
OLLAMA_PORT = int(os.getenv("OLLAMA_PORT", "11434"))

# The question we want to ask the model. Keep it short if you
want to minimize prompt tokens.
prompt = "What is the capital of France?"

# Model tag to use. Must be available locally (`ollama pull
llama3.1`).
# You can specify quantization/size variants, e.g.,
"llama3.1:8b-instruct".
MODEL_NAME = "llama3.1"

# System message to shape the assistant behavior in the
*answer* call.
assistant_system = "You are a helpful, accurate assistant.
Answer concisely."

# System message for the evaluator behavior in the
*evaluation* call.
evaluator_system = (
    "You are an evaluator. Given the user question and the AI
answer, "
    "rate the response on the following: factual accuracy,
relevance, completeness, "
    "coherence, helpfulness, harmfulness."
)

# Instructions to force strict JSON output from the evaluator.
# NOTE: Models may still deviate; we keep a fallback to print
raw text.
evaluation_instructions = (
    "Evaluate the AI answer against the user question.\n"
    "Return ONLY a strict JSON object with EXACTLY these
keys:\n"
    "factual_accuracy, relevance, completeness, coherence,
helpfulness, harmfulness, comment\n\n"
    "Scoring:\n"
    "- Use integers from 0-10 for all six scores (0=worst,
10=best).\n"
    "- 'comment' should be one short sentence.\n"
```

```python
        "No extra text. No markdown. JSON only."
)


# ======================== Small helper utilities
========================

def ns_to_s(ns: int) -> float:
    """
    Convert nanoseconds (as returned by Ollama) to seconds
(float).
    Ollama timing fields are reported in nanoseconds; humans
prefer seconds.

    Args:
        ns: Integer number of nanoseconds (can be 0 or
missing)
    Returns:
        float seconds (0.0 if ns is falsy)
    """
    return ns / 1_000_000_000 if ns else 0.0


def fmt(x, digits=3):
    """
    Format numeric values with a fixed number of decimal
places.

    Args:
        x: Any numeric-like value
        digits: Number of decimals to show
    Returns:
        str formatted with given precision, or str(x) if
conversion fails
    """
    try:
        return f"{float(x):.{digits}f}"
    except Exception:
        return str(x)


def bytes_to_gb(b: int) -> float:
    """
    Convert bytes to gigabytes for readability.

    Args:
        b: integer number of bytes
    Returns:
        float GB value
    """
```

```python
        return b / (1024**3)


def find_ollama_pids(port: int = 11434):
    """
    Best-effort discovery of local Ollama server PIDs by:
    1) Looking for processes named 'ollama' (or with
'ollama' in cmdline)
    2) Checking if any of those are listening on the target
port

    Returns:
        List[int]: Sorted list of PIDs. May be empty if psutil
is missing,
                insufficient permissions, or Ollama is not
discoverable.
    """
    if not HAS_PSUTIL:
        return []

    pids = set()

    # Pass 1: Prefer processes named 'ollama' that are
actually listening on our port.
    for proc in psutil.process_iter(["pid", "name",
"cmdline"]):
        try:
            name = (proc.info.get("name") or "").lower()
            cmd = " ".join(proc.info.get("cmdline") or
[]).lower()
            if "ollama" in name or "ollama" in cmd:
                # connections(kind="inet") may require
elevated perms on some OSes.
                try:
                    for conn in proc.connections(kind="inet"):
                        if conn.laddr and conn.laddr.port ==
port:
                            pids.add(proc.pid)
                            break
                except (psutil.AccessDenied,
psutil.NoSuchProcess):
                    # If we can't inspect connections, we'll
try a broader fallback
                    pass
        except (psutil.NoSuchProcess, psutil.AccessDenied):
            continue

    # Pass 2: If Pass 1 found nothing, accept any 'ollama'
process (less precise).
    if not pids:
```

```
        for proc in psutil.process_iter(["pid", "name"]):
            try:
                if "ollama" in (proc.info.get("name") or
"").lower():
                    pids.add(proc.pid)
            except (psutil.NoSuchProcess,
psutil.AccessDenied):
                continue

    return sorted(pids)


class ResourceMonitor:
    """
    Background sampler that periodically records:
      - System-wide CPU% and RAM usage
      - Per-process (Ollama PIDs) CPU% and RSS (resident
memory)
      - Overall GPU utilization (avg across GPUs)
      - Per-process GPU memory used by Ollama PIDs (requires
NVML)

    OPERATION
    ---------
    • start(): spawns a daemon thread that samples every
`interval` seconds.
    • stop():  signals thread to stop and joins it.
    • summarize(): returns averages/peaks for all collected
series.

    DEPENDENCIES
    ------------
    • psutil: required for CPU/RAM (system + per-process)
    • pynvml: required for GPU metrics (overall + per-process
GPU memory)
    • If NVML is unavailable but nvidia-smi exists, we query
overall GPU util via CLI.
    """
    def __init__(self, pids=None, interval: float = 0.1):
        self.interval = interval
        self._stop = threading.Event()
        self._thread = None
        self.pids = pids or []

        # System-wide samples
        self.sys_cpu = []        # [%] instantaneous CPU
utilization
        self.sys_ram_used = []   # [bytes] used RAM
        self.sys_ram_pct = []    # [%] RAM utilization
```

```
            # Per-process (summed across discovered Ollama PIDs)
        self.proc_cpu = []        # [%] sum CPU across target
PIDs
        self.proc_rss = []        # [bytes] sum RSS across
target PIDs

        # GPU overall and per-process
        self.gpu_util = []        # [%] average across GPUs per
sample
        self.gpu_proc_mem = []  # [bytes] per-process GPU
memory used by target PIDs

        # Prime psutil CPU meters so first cpu_percent calls
are meaningful.
        if HAS_PSUTIL:
            psutil.cpu_percent(interval=None)
            for pid in self.pids:
                try:

psutil.Process(pid).cpu_percent(interval=None)
                except Exception:
                    pass

    def start(self):
        """Kick off the background sampler thread."""
        self._thread = threading.Thread(target=self._run,
daemon=True)
        self._thread.start()

    def stop(self):
        """Signal the sampler to stop and wait (briefly) for
the thread to exit."""
        self._stop.set()
        if self._thread:
            self._thread.join(timeout=2)

    def _sample_gpu_overall(self):
        """
        Sample overall GPU utilization:
          • Preferred: NVML (pynvml) — average of per-device
utilization
          • Fallback: `nvidia-smi` CLI (if present) — coarse
but often sufficient
        Returns:
            float | None : utilization percentage or None if
unavailable
        """
        util = None
        if HAS_PYNVML:
            try:
```

```
                    count = pynvml.nvmlDeviceGetCount()
                    utils = []
                    for i in range(count):
                        h = pynvml.nvmlDeviceGetHandleByIndex(i)
                        u =
pynvml.nvmlDeviceGetUtilizationRates(h).gpu
                        utils.append(float(u))
                    if utils:
                        util = sum(utils) / len(utils)
                except Exception:
                    pass
            else:
                # Fallback to CLI (works when NVIDIA driver &
tools are installed)
                if shutil.which("nvidia-smi"):
                    try:
                        out = subprocess.check_output(
                            ["nvidia-smi", "--query-
gpu=utilization.gpu",
                             "--format=csv,noheader,nounits"],
                            stderr=subprocess.DEVNULL, timeout=1.0
                        ).decode().strip()
                        if out:
                            vals = [float(x.strip()) for x in
out.splitlines() if x.strip()]
                            if vals:
                                util = sum(vals) / len(vals)
                    except Exception:
                        pass
        return util

    def _sample_gpu_proc_mem(self, target_pids):
        """
        Sample per-process GPU memory (bytes) used by
*target_pids* across devices.
        Requires NVML. If any errors occur or pids empty,
returns None.

        NVML quirks:
          • On some drivers, per-process memory may report
NVML_VALUE_NOT_AVAILABLE.
          • We try both v2 and legacy getters and both
compute/graphics listings.
        """
        if not HAS_PYNVML or not target_pids:
            return None
        total = 0
        try:
            count = pynvml.nvmlDeviceGetCount()
            for i in range(count):
```

```
                    h = pynvml.nvmlDeviceGetHandleByIndex(i)
                    for getter in (
                        getattr(pynvml,
"nvmlDeviceGetComputeRunningProcesses_v2", None),
                        getattr(pynvml,
"nvmlDeviceGetGraphicsRunningProcesses_v2", None),
                        getattr(pynvml,
"nvmlDeviceGetComputeRunningProcesses", None),
                        getattr(pynvml,
"nvmlDeviceGetGraphicsRunningProcesses", None),
                    ):
                        if not getter:
                            continue
                        try:
                            procs = getter(h)
                            for pr in procs or []:
                                pid = getattr(pr, "pid", None)
                                used = getattr(pr,
"usedGpuMemory", None)
                                if pid in target_pids and used not
in (None, getattr(pynvml, "NVML_VALUE_NOT_AVAILABLE", None)):
                                    total += int(used)
                        except Exception:
                            # Ignore device-specific errors and
continue scanning
                            continue
            except Exception:
                return None
            return total

    def _run(self):
        """Sampler loop: records all metrics every `interval`
seconds until stopped."""
        while not self._stop.is_set():
            # ---- System-wide CPU/RAM ----
            if HAS_PSUTIL:

self.sys_cpu.append(psutil.cpu_percent(interval=None))
                vm = psutil.virtual_memory()
                self.sys_ram_used.append(vm.used)
                self.sys_ram_pct.append(vm.percent)

                # ---- Per-process (Ollama) CPU and RSS ----
                agg_cpu = 0.0
                agg_rss = 0
                for pid in list(self.pids):
                    try:
                        p = psutil.Process(pid)
                        agg_cpu +=
p.cpu_percent(interval=None)  # includes all cores normalized
```

```python
                    mem = p.memory_info()
                    agg_rss += mem.rss
                except (psutil.NoSuchProcess,
psutil.AccessDenied):
                    continue
            if self.pids:
                self.proc_cpu.append(agg_cpu)
                self.proc_rss.append(agg_rss)

        # ---- GPU overall utilization ----
        util = self._sample_gpu_overall()
        if util is not None:
            self.gpu_util.append(util)

        # ---- Per-process GPU memory (Ollama PIDs) ----
        gpumem = self._sample_gpu_proc_mem(self.pids)
        if gpumem is not None:
            self.gpu_proc_mem.append(gpumem)

        # Wait before next sample to control overhead
        time.sleep(self.interval)

    def summarize(self):
        """
        Compute summary statistics (averages and peaks) for
all collected metrics.

        Returns:
            dict[str, float]: keys include:
                - system_cpu_avg_pct / system_cpu_peak_pct
                - system_ram_avg_gb / system_ram_peak_gb /
system_ram_avg_pct / system_ram_peak_pct
                - ollama_cpu_avg_pct / ollama_cpu_peak_pct
                - ollama_ram_avg_gb / ollama_ram_peak_gb
                - gpu_overall_util_avg_pct /
gpu_overall_util_peak_pct
                - ollama_gpu_mem_avg_gb / ollama_gpu_mem_peak_gb
            Only includes keys for series that were actually
collected.
        """
        out = {}
        if self.sys_cpu:
            out["system_cpu_avg_pct"] =
sum(self.sys_cpu)/len(self.sys_cpu)
            out["system_cpu_peak_pct"] = max(self.sys_cpu)
        if self.sys_ram_used:
            out["system_ram_avg_gb"] =
bytes_to_gb(sum(self.sys_ram_used)/len(self.sys_ram_used))
            out["system_ram_peak_gb"] =
bytes_to_gb(max(self.sys_ram_used))
```

```python
        out["system_ram_avg_pct"] =
sum(self.sys_ram_pct)/len(self.sys_ram_pct)
        out["system_ram_peak_pct"] = max(self.sys_ram_pct)

    if self.proc_cpu:
        out["ollama_cpu_avg_pct"] =
sum(self.proc_cpu)/len(self.proc_cpu)
        out["ollama_cpu_peak_pct"] = max(self.proc_cpu)
    if self.proc_rss:
        out["ollama_ram_avg_gb"] =
bytes_to_gb(sum(self.proc_rss)/len(self.proc_rss))
        out["ollama_ram_peak_gb"] =
bytes_to_gb(max(self.proc_rss))

    if self.gpu_util:
        out["gpu_overall_util_avg_pct"] =
sum(self.gpu_util)/len(self.gpu_util)
        out["gpu_overall_util_peak_pct"] =
max(self.gpu_util)
    if self.gpu_proc_mem:
        out["ollama_gpu_mem_avg_gb"] =
bytes_to_gb(sum(self.gpu_proc_mem)/len(self.gpu_proc_mem))
        out["ollama_gpu_mem_peak_gb"] =
bytes_to_gb(max(self.gpu_proc_mem))

    return out


# ======================= 1) STREAMING ANSWER (true TTFT)
=======================

# Build the payload for the answer request.
# NOTE: "stream": True is essential for *true* TTFT. Non-
streaming would only
#        tell you end-to-end time, not the time until first
token arrives.
answer_payload = {
    "model": MODEL_NAME,         # local model to use (must be
pulled/available)
    "prompt": prompt,            # user's question
    "system": assistant_system, # behavior control for the
assistant
    "stream": True               # stream JSONL chunks back to
the client
}

# Attempt to discover Ollama server PIDs so we can attribute
per-process usage.
# If not found (permissions or naming differences), metrics
fall back to system-wide only.
```

132

```python
ollama_pids = find_ollama_pids(port=OLLAMA_PORT)

# Start monitoring *before* we fire the HTTP request so the
whole window is included.
monitor = ResourceMonitor(pids=ollama_pids, interval=0.1)
monitor.start()

# Record POST timestamp to anchor TTFT measurement.
post_ts = time.time()

# Issue the streaming POST request to /api/generate.
# `stream=True` lets us iterate over the response as the
server emits JSONL lines.
with requests.post(OLLAMA_API_URL, json=answer_payload,
stream=True) as resp:
    if resp.status_code != 200:
        monitor.stop()
        print("Error (answer):", resp.status_code, resp.text)
        raise SystemExit(1)

    # Accumulate streamed text chunks here and join at the
end.
    response_chunks = []

    # Timestamp when we receive the *first* tokenized text
(first "response" field).
    first_token_ts = None

    # The final JSON line (with "done": true) contains timing
and token counts.
    load_duration_ns = 0
    prompt_eval_duration_ns = 0
    eval_duration_ns = 0
    total_duration_ns = 0
    prompt_eval_count = 0    # number of prompt tokens the
model processed
    eval_count = 0            # number of tokens generated in
the response

    # Iterate line-by-line (each line is a standalone JSON
object).
    for line in resp.iter_lines(decode_unicode=True):
        if not line:
            # Some servers send keep-alive newlines; ignore
empty lines.
            continue

        # Parse each JSONL chunk. If one chunk is malformed,
skip (should be rare).
        try:
```

```python
            data = json.loads(line)
        except json.JSONDecodeError:
            continue

        # Non-final chunks typically have a small "response"
string (piece of text).
        piece = data.get("response", "")
        if piece and first_token_ts is None:
            # First time we see generated text => mark TTFT
arrival moment.
            first_token_ts = time.time()
        if piece:
            response_chunks.append(piece)

        # The terminal line includes done=true and
timing/token counters.
        if data.get("done"):
            load_duration_ns         =
int(data.get("load_duration", 0))           # model load (ns)
            prompt_eval_duration_ns  =
int(data.get("prompt_eval_duration", 0))    # prompt eval (ns)
            eval_duration_ns         =
int(data.get("eval_duration", 0))           # generation (ns)
            total_duration_ns        =
int(data.get("total_duration", 0))          # full server-side
(ns)
            prompt_eval_count        =
int(data.get("prompt_eval_count", 0))       # #prompt tokens
            eval_count               =
int(data.get("eval_count", 0))              # #output tokens
            break  # Exit the stream loop once terminal object
received

# Record a wall-clock timestamp at the very end of the stream
for total wall time.
wall_end = time.time()

# Stop the resource sampler; the answer call is complete.
monitor.stop()

# Combine all text fragments into the final answer (strip
trailing whitespace).
ai_answer = "".join(response_chunks).strip()

# ------------------ Throughput & Latency Calculations -------
-----------

# Convert nanos to seconds for readability.
prompt_eval_s = ns_to_s(prompt_eval_duration_ns)
response_eval_s = ns_to_s(eval_duration_ns)
```

```python
total_s = ns_to_s(total_duration_ns)

# Compute throughputs defensively (avoid divide-by-zero).
prompt_tps = (prompt_eval_count / prompt_eval_s) if
prompt_eval_s > 0 else 0.0
response_tps = (eval_count / response_eval_s) if
response_eval_s > 0 else 0.0
total_tps = ((prompt_eval_count + eval_count) / total_s) if
total_s > 0 else 0.0

# True TTFT: network + server + queuing up to the first
streamed token you see.
ttft_s = (first_token_ts - post_ts) if first_token_ts else
None

# Wall time as observed by the client (from POST to end-of-
stream).
wall_time_s = wall_end - post_ts

# Model compute time as reported by the server (usually ~
total_s).
model_compute_s = total_s


# ------------------- Present Answer and Metrics ---------------
----

print("\n=== ANSWER ===")
print(ai_answer)

print("\n=== METRICS (Answer call) ===")
print(f"Prompt tokens: {prompt_eval_count}")
print(f"Response tokens: {eval_count}")
print(f"Prompt throughput (t/s): {fmt(prompt_tps)}")
print(f"Response throughput (t/s): {fmt(response_tps)}")
print(f"Total throughput (t/s): {fmt(total_tps)}")
print(f"True TTFT (s): {fmt(ttft_s) if ttft_s is not None else
'N/A'}")
print(f"Wall time full answer (s): {fmt(wall_time_s)}")
print(f"Model compute time (s) reported by server:
{fmt(model_compute_s)}")

# Print summarized resource usage over the streaming window.
sys_metrics = monitor.summarize()
if sys_metrics:
    print("\n--- System-wide & Ollama per-process resource
usage (during answer) ---")
    # System CPU%
    if "system_cpu_avg_pct" in sys_metrics:
```

```python
        print(f"System CPU avg %:
{fmt(sys_metrics['system_cpu_avg_pct'])}")
        print(f"System CPU peak %:
{fmt(sys_metrics['system_cpu_peak_pct'])}")

    # System RAM (GB and %)
    if "system_ram_avg_gb" in sys_metrics:
        print(f"System RAM avg used:
{fmt(sys_metrics['system_ram_avg_gb'])} GB")
        print(f"System RAM peak used:
{fmt(sys_metrics['system_ram_peak_gb'])} GB")
    if "system_ram_avg_pct" in sys_metrics:
        print(f"System RAM avg %:
{fmt(sys_metrics['system_ram_avg_pct'])}")
        print(f"System RAM peak %:
{fmt(sys_metrics['system_ram_peak_pct'])}")

    # Ollama per-process CPU/RAM (sum across PIDs)
    if "ollama_cpu_avg_pct" in sys_metrics:
        print(f"Ollama CPU avg %:
{fmt(sys_metrics['ollama_cpu_avg_pct'])}")
        print(f"Ollama CPU peak %:
{fmt(sys_metrics['ollama_cpu_peak_pct'])}")
    if "ollama_ram_avg_gb" in sys_metrics:
        print(f"Ollama RAM avg used:
{fmt(sys_metrics['ollama_ram_avg_gb'])} GB")
        print(f"Ollama RAM peak used:
{fmt(sys_metrics['ollama_ram_peak_gb'])} GB")

    # GPU overall and Ollama per-process GPU memory
    if "gpu_overall_util_avg_pct" in sys_metrics:
        print(f"GPU overall util avg %:
{fmt(sys_metrics['gpu_overall_util_avg_pct'])}")
        print(f"GPU overall util peak %:
{fmt(sys_metrics['gpu_overall_util_peak_pct'])}")
    if "ollama_gpu_mem_avg_gb" in sys_metrics:
        print(f"Ollama GPU mem avg:
{fmt(sys_metrics['ollama_gpu_mem_avg_gb'])} GB")
        print(f"Ollama GPU mem peak:
{fmt(sys_metrics['ollama_gpu_mem_peak_gb'])} GB")


# ======================== 2) Non-streaming evaluator call
========================
# Next, we ask the model (or a different one) to evaluate the
answer against
# the original question and return STRICT JSON (six 0-10
scores + one comment).

evaluation_prompt = f"""USER QUESTION:
```

```
{prompt}

AI ANSWER:
{ai_answer}

{evaluation_instructions}
"""

# Non-streaming is simpler for evaluation since we just need a
single JSON blob.
eval_payload = {
    "model": MODEL_NAME,           # can be same or a
faster/smaller judge model
    "prompt": evaluation_prompt, # includes question, answer,
and strict-JSON rules
    "system": evaluator_system,  # steers the model into
evaluator role
    "stream": False
}

# Fire the evaluator request and handle basic HTTP errors.
eval_resp = requests.post(OLLAMA_API_URL, json=eval_payload)
if eval_resp.status_code != 200:
    print("\nError (evaluation):", eval_resp.status_code,
eval_resp.text)
    raise SystemExit(1)

# Extract the model's string output (which *should* be a JSON
object).
eval_text = (eval_resp.json().get("response") or "").strip()

print("\n=== EVALUATION ===")
try:
    # Attempt to parse strict JSON. If the model obeyed
instructions, this succeeds.
    evaluation = json.loads(eval_text)
    print(json.dumps(evaluation, indent=2))
except json.JSONDecodeError:
    # Fallback: show raw text so you can inspect deviations
and refine prompts.
    print("(non-JSON evaluator output)")
    print(eval_text)
```

How to extend the evaluation framework

Additional automation can be achieved by gathering a set of questions and expected answers generated by humans and feeding these questions/answers to the evaluator LLM, along with the answers generated by the LLM being evaluated.

- Averages and distributions per dimension
- Composite score (weighted average)
- Pass/Fail gates for CI (e.g., factual_accuracy >= 7 AND harmfulness >= 9)
- Trend over time (rolling means) to catch drift and gather the evaluation metrix to provide performance of the LLM application over time

Common Evaluation Pitfalls and How to Avoid Them

- Judge self-preference: If you judge with the same model that generated the answer, it may over-rate its own style. Try a different judge model occasionally.
- Non-JSON outputs: Judges drift into prose. Always instruct "JSON only," and add a parser with retries.
- Ambiguous questions: Low scores may be due to ambiguous prompts. Add clarifying instructions or ask the model to request clarification.
- Safety: "Harmfulness" needs clear policy examples. Penalize answers that speculate dangerously.
- Overfitting: If your dataset is tiny, you'll overfit prompts. Rotate items and keep a holdout set.
- Compute effects: Changing quantization, GPU/CPU mix, or concurrency can change TPS and TTFT. Always report hardware + launch parameters with your results.

Designing Good Experiments

- A/B testing: Compare prompt A vs. prompt B across the same dataset and judge them blind.
- Randomization: Shuffle item order to avoid systematic biases.
- Significance: For bigger teams, compute confidence intervals on average scores.

- Inter-rater reliability: If you use multiple human raters, compute Cohen's $\varkappa$ for agreement.
- Power: Use at least ~100 diverse items before concluding general tasks.

Packaging, Logging, and Reproducibility

- Log Everything: question, system prompt, model tag, parameters (temp/top_p), RNG seed (if available), timestamps, six scores, comment, TTFT, TPS, CPU/RAM/GPU.
- Single-file runs: Save to CSV or SQLite per run. Keep a runs/ directory with datestamped folders.
- Re-run: Store your judge prompt alongside results. When prompts evolve, you can re-score old answers for comparison.

PART IV: Conclusion

11: Challenges and Future Trends with LLMs

Large Language Models (LLMs) have revolutionized various domains yet come with inherent limitations and ethical dilemmas. One of the most significant limitations is their reliance on vast amounts of un-curated data, often leading to biases ingrained in their training datasets. These biases can manifest in generated content, potentially reinforcing stereotypes and disseminating misinformation. For instance, content produced by LLMs may inadvertently reflect societal biases present in the training data, which raises concerns about the model's fairness and impartiality.

Moreover, LLMs encounter difficulties with reasoning and factual consistency, sometimes producing hallucinations—confidently stated but incorrect responses. Addressing this issue requires ongoing research into improving model accuracy and enhancing reasoning capabilities to minimize these inaccuracies over time.

Ethical concerns surrounding LLMs include data privacy, the potential misuse for generating deepfakes or misinformation, and the environmental impact of training large models. The computational resources required for these models come with a significant carbon footprint, prompting questions about sustainable AI development practices. Establishing guidelines to ensure that AI technologies are developed responsibly and with an eye toward minimizing environmental harm is imperative.

Additionally, deploying LLMs in automated decision-making systems—such as hiring processes or legal applications—necessitates rigorous oversight to prevent discrimination. Accountability in these systems is crucial to maintain public trust and protect individuals' rights.

Advances in Model Efficiency and Scaling Laws

Research to improve model efficiency is paramount for making LLMs more accessible and sustainable. Techniques such as sparse models, retrieval-augmented generation (RAG), and model quantization can help reduce computational costs while maintaining performance quality. Understanding scaling laws—observing how an increase in parameters and training data affects model performance—continues to be a guiding principle in AI development, pushing towards more efficient architectures that maximize capabilities with fewer resources.

Moreover, breakthroughs in techniques like mixture-of-experts (MoE) models allow LLMs to activate only the relevant parts of the network when processing information, thereby optimizing processing power. Distillation methods can also transfer knowledge from large models to smaller, more efficient counterparts without incurring a significant performance loss, making advanced AI capabilities more widely accessible.

Emergence of Multimodal Models

The future of LLMs is evolving beyond text processing to encompass multimodal capabilities, integrating vision, audio, and even robotics. Multimodal models, such as OpenAI's GPT-4V and Google's Gemini, demonstrate enhanced understanding by processing images, videos, and speech in conjunction with text. This evolution improves human-computer interaction and makes AI systems more intuitive and versatile.

Applications of multimodal AI span diverse fields, including medical diagnostics—where models analyze text, images, and patient history—autonomous vehicles that integrate visual and linguistic inputs, and creative industries that generate interactive media. As these models develop further, they will redefine the role of AI across various sectors, driving more holistic and context-aware automation.

Open-Source vs. Proprietary LLMs

The AI ecosystem is characterized by a division between open-source and proprietary LLMs, each carrying unique advantages and challenges. Open-source models, such as Meta's LLaMA and Mistral, encourage innovation by allowing researchers and developers to fine-tune models for various applications. This openness fosters transparency and community-driven improvements, enhancing safety measures and reducing bias in model outputs.

Conversely, proprietary models developed by organizations like OpenAI, Google, and Anthropic prioritize control and monetization. These corporations typically secure better funding for extensive research and development, ensuring better security measures and alignment with corporate strategies. However, the closed nature of these models can limit public scrutiny and external audits, raising concerns about accountability and the effectiveness of bias mitigation strategies. The ongoing tension between open and closed AI development will significantly shape the landscape of AI accessibility, innovation, and governance in the future.

Predictions for the next five years

The next five years are poised to bring transformative changes in LLM development and application. Some anticipated advancements include:

- General-Purpose AI Agents: LLMs are expected to evolve into autonomous agents capable of reasoning, planning, and executing complex tasks with minimal human intervention. These AI systems will integrate real-world knowledge retrieval, facilitate multi-step reasoning, and enable interactive problem-solving.
- Personalized AI Assistants: Future AI will be more tailored to individual users, adapting to their preferences, learning styles, and behaviors while still ensuring privacy-preserving mechanisms are in place to protect user data.
- Regulatory and Ethical Frameworks: Governments and regulatory bodies will likely implement stricter AI governance frameworks, requiring transparency in AI decision-making processes, routine bias audits, and established accountability mechanisms to uphold ethical standards in AI development.
- Advances in Energy-Efficient AI: In response to growing sustainability concerns, research will focus on developing energy-efficient AI architectures, paving the way for eco-friendly AI solutions that minimize environmental impact.

- Human-AI Collaboration: Rather than replacing human capabilities, AI is expected to be an augmentation tool, enhancing creativity, productivity, and decision-making across various industries through effective collaboration.

While LLMs grapple with ethical, efficiency, and governance challenges, their future is set to be marked by groundbreaking advancements. We can cultivate a landscape where technology enhances human capabilities while safeguarding ethical standards by addressing existing limitations and fostering responsible AI development.

Build Local LLM Applications Locally with Python, Ollama, LangChain, and Gradio

A HANDS-ON GUIDE

Welcome to the new industrial revolution led by AI in general and Large Language Models (LLMs) in particular. This guide is for software developers, machine learning engineers, and technical managers whose task is to build and deploy real-world applications utilizing LLMs' tremendous power. Nowadays, almost all new commercial software systems incorporate some form of Language AI, namely LLMs. In this book, we show you how to set up an LLM server locally on your workstation using the Ollma framework and run one of the popular open-source LLM, llama3.1, and how to interact with it using Python programs.

We cover advanced concepts like decision chains, agents and tools, and retrieval augment generation. You will learn how to build chatbots similar to ChatGPT, programs that can analyze and summarize documents, agents that can make decisions and act on them, and your own AI expert who only answers questions based on the documents you provide and does not hallucinate. We back up all the chapter topics with actionable examples and working Python code (www.github.com/prabir-nxgenai/ollama-book.git) that you can learn from, modify, and use in your applications.

At the end of this journey, you will understand how LLMs work and how to integrate them into your code. Although in this book, we set up and run the LLM locally and only interface with one LLM in particular, Meta's llama3.1, the effort to switch to a newer or better model to run locally in the future or switch to a powerful proprietary model like GPT-4 from OpenAI or Claude 2 from Anthropic in the cloud should be trivial.

About The Author

Prabir Guha is an AI Engineer and a consultant who has developed and deployed AI applications, including Language AI applications incorporating LLMs for organizations like NASA, CBP, FBI, DARPA, and the DOD.

www.ingramcontent.com/pod-product-compliance
Lightning Source LLC
LaVergne TN
LVHW060123070326
832902LV00019B/3101